MW01061616

# FIGHT BACK

*Moving from deliverance to dominion*

Vladimir Savchuk

# Dedication

To all soldiers in the spiritual battle.

# Table of Contents

# Foreword

I thank God for Pastor Vladimir Savchuk for having the heart and courage to expose the enemy through this powerful book called *Fight Back*.

This book has many facets of being victorious and an overcomer. *Fight Back* is an amazing book that will help so many people understand the wiles and schemes of the enemy. It will also set many people free from fear and many other attacks to live a victorious life.

One of the things that stood out is this amazing statement: "Bondage makes you a slave; battle makes you a soldier." It's time to be a soldier for Christ, and this book will be a good tool to add to your spiritual warfare collection.

Evangelist John Ramirez,

Author of *Out of the Devil's Cauldron*, *Unmasking the Devil*, and *Armed and Dangerous*.

# Deliverance is not the Goal

For as long as I can remember, I was always afraid of the dark. Since I was the oldest in my family, I was the first child to have my own bedroom. But I was afraid when the lights were turned off. Even when I was a youth pastor, having to lock up the church late at night, I would run from the door to my car with my heart beating wildly. I would check the back seat just to make sure that Jack the Ripper wasn't sitting there waiting to kill me.

After I got married, my wife and I moved into an apartment. Like any normal apartment, there was no ceiling light in the living room. One Saturday night as we were having dinner in the kitchen, I started to feel something was not right in the living room. In fact, I thought I saw a spirit-being quickly flashing in the dark, and it made the hair on the back of my neck stand up. As I turned away from looking into the living room to look at my wife, I squeezed her hand really tightly. Lana noticed something was not right. She asked me if everything was okay. Of course, I wasn't about to admit that I just got scared of the dark.

When dinner was over, she turned off the kitchen light, and we went to the office where she would paint and I would finish the final touches on my sermon. Guess what

# Introduction

my sermon was about? Victory over the devil! I was preparing a sermon on victory, and yet I was scared of the
dark. This fear of the dark had been in my life for as long
as I could remember. I even asked God to remove it, but
it always seemed like God wanted me to resist it.

Suddenly out of nowhere, my wife asked me if I would
go and bring her some water from the kitchen. Now keep
in mind this meant that I would have to go down the hall-
way, through the living room, and then into the kitchen
with all the lights off. This may sound funny to some, but
I was scared to death. I felt that something creepy was in
the living room, and it would kill me if I went in there. I
tried to persuade my wife to get her own water, but she
insisted that she couldn't because she was painting. I
should just go and bring her water.

I decided that, since there was no way I would tell
Lana that I was afraid in my own apartment, I would go
and get the water, even if I had to die in my living room.
My plan was simple. I would run as fast as I could to reach
the light switch in the kitchen, turn on the light, get the
water, and then leave the lights on. She would later turn
them off before we went to sleep. I was about to leave the
room and race to the light switch when I heard the Holy
Spirit say, "Do NOT turn on the light; you are the light." I
felt him speak loudly to my pounding heart, "I will not remove your fear of darkness because I have empowered
YOU to resist it." Yet in my mind, it was like, "that's easy
for you to say God, but here I am scared and I am going to
die." Well, I decided, enough is enough! My time had
come. I had to face what I've been fleeing from all my life.
With my heart thumping like crazy and feeling every
ounce of fear, I walked into the living room. Without turn-
ing on the light, I positioned myself in the middle of the
living room and this is what came out of my mouth:

# Fight Back

"Darkness or whatever you are, you have no place in this house anymore. I pay the bills here so get out now!" Faith was released in my spirit. Immediately, fear left and whatever demon was masquerading behind that endless fear was gone---forever. I have never had that kind of fear again. My fear of the dark has become a thing of the past.

I prayed for deliverance from fear, but God had another plan. He wanted me to exercise the undiscovered dominion over the fear that I already had in Jesus. I wanted freedom from fear; God wanted me to fight it. I wanted God to remove it; God wanted me to resist it.

Now I can see there is a shift taking place in the Body of Christ where the Holy Spirit is empowering everyday believers to operate in the authority that is already theirs through Jesus Christ. *"Let the high praises of God be in their mouth, and a two-edged sword in their hand; To execute vengeance on the nations, and punishments on the peoples; To bind their kings with chains, and their nobles with fetters of iron; To execute on them the written judgment— This honor have all His saints. Praise the LORD!"* (Psalm 149:6-9).

God wants us to have praises in our mouth and His sword in our hands. Spiritual warfare doesn't work if our mouth is full of complaining and admitting defeat. Our mouth speaks or reveals what is in our hearts. We were created to worship, and we are now called to engage in warfare. Warfare and worship go together. The high praises of God must be coming out of our mouth and our hands must securely hold onto the double-edged sword which is none other than the Word of our God (Hebrews 4:12). This sword of the Spirit is to bind and execute punishment on the enemy. We are used to only being delivered from bondage. Instead, God is now preparing a mighty generation to put the enemy in bondage, to put chains on the forces of darkness through the authority of Jesus' name.

As Jesus said, *"How can one enter a strong man's house and plunder his goods, unless he first binds the strong man? And then he will plunder his house"* (Matthew 12:28), the roles have been reversed. The enemy used to bind us; now we can bind him through the victory of almighty Jesus who is invincible.

This is more than just being freed from the enemy; this is being empowered to successfully fight the enemy. I love this part: *"This honor have all his saints."* Victory, dominion, and a fighting spirit are an honor. This honor to take dominion, to trample upon forces of darkness, to bind the enemy has been given to all his saints. This honor belongs to all of God's children. Victory is not just for a few but for all. Authority over the enemy belongs to all believers. *"Whatever you bind on earth shall be bound."* (Matthew 18:18).

God is building up a dynamic church that will not tolerate the torments of the devil but instead will torment his demons. The time has come for demons to cry out as they did during the days of Jesus, *"Have You come here to torment us before the time?"* (Matthew 8:29). I'm sure you know some people who are tormented by demons, who are in bondage and in desperate need of deliverance. But did you know that you are the one called and entrusted to bind the enemy, to bring torment to demons just as Jesus did? You were called not just to receive deliverance but to walk in dominion. Don't just wait for God to cast out every enemy, but walk in the power of the Holy Spirit to actively resist whatever He has not yet removed.

The first book I wrote, *Break Free,* focused on how to get free and stay free from Satan's power. Most of the book emphasized the reality of the spiritual realm and how to obtain freedom through Jesus. *Break Free* has been translated into several languages and I have received many amazing testimonies from all over the world of healing, freedom, and salvation.

In this current book, I want to build on that foundation of deliverance and to go one step further, showing that God's ultimate goal is not just deliverance but dominion. As a pastor, I lead the Hungry Generation Church where we pray for healing and deliverance every week. Once a year, we hold an international conference called Raised to Deliver where people come from all around the world to receive their touch from Jesus. However, my heart is broken for the folks who get delivered but don't learn how to walk in victory, and soon they're back again seeking deliverance. They constantly feel like there is more that needs to be cast out of them. I don't want to downplay the need for a total, complete deliverance; I want to highlight the importance of walking in victory as the only way people can get their full deliverance.

There is a danger in not moving toward absolute dominion after receiving deliverance. It can cause us to end up seeking deliverance again and again. We begin to go from deliverance to deliverance, instead of from deliverance to dominion. The United States of America, the country where I am currently residing, has a huge problem with bondage. We have about 5% of the world's population yet have around 25% of the world's incarcerated prisoners.[1] Having so many prisoners in prison is a gigantic problem, but prisoners returning to the same prison is an even worse crisis in the USA. A study from the Bureau

---

[1] Lee, Michelle. "Does the United States Really Have 5 Percent of the World's Population and One Quarter of the World's Prisoners?" *The Washington Post*, WP Company, 30 Apr. 2015, 7:00am, www.washingtonpost.com/news/fact-checker/wp/2015/04/30/does-the-united-states-really-have-five-percent-of-worlds-population-and-one-quarter-of-the-worlds-prisoners/.

of Justice Statistics called "Recidivism of Prisoners Released in 30 States in 2005: Patterns from 2005 to 2010" found that 76% of prisoners released from state prisons were arrested again within 5 years of their release.[2] This study tracked 69,279 prisoners for 5 years and found that most of them were arrested again within their first few years of freedom. When I used to preach in jail, security guards would tell me that most of the men there were not there for the first time. And for many of them, that would not be their last time being imprisoned either.

Instead of moving from deliverance to deliverance, God intended for us to move from deliverance to dominion. Let's take Israel for example. God didn't plan for them to keep going back to Egypt for more deliverance after things got hard in the wilderness. Instead, led by the cloud each day and by fire at night, God expected them to move forward to become fearless soldiers. God was not just taking slaves out of the land of bondage, but He was leading them to conquer the land of promise. Israel was tempted to go back to Egypt many times. They talked about it, complained about it, and even threatened God and Moses about it. At times, life in bondage seemed better than a life of freedom in the desert. They failed to understand that even though freedom is free, learning to walk in victory takes time, effort, adjusting, and training.

God's plan of getting Israel out of Egypt was not the final goal. It was only a means to the goal. The goal was for them to take possession of the Promised Land; God didn't just give it to them. In Egypt, they received deliverance by doing very little, but in the Promised Land, they would have to fight to take possession of it and keep what

---

[2] Durose, Matthew R., et al. "Recidivism Of Prisoners Released In 30 States In 2005: Patterns From 2005 To 2010 - Update." *Bureau of Justice Statistics (BJS)*, 22 Apr. 2014, www.bjs.gov/index.cfm?ty=pbdetail&iid=4986%2B.

was promised. In fact, the children of Israel only possessed what they fought for, not what they wished and hoped for. What was true for them is also true of us today. God delivers us from the cruel Pharaoh, but He expects us to conquer the wicked Philistines. The Promised Land was different from Egypt. The Israelites were delivered from Egypt, but the Promised Land required taking dominion. That's what Israel did and that's what we must learn to do as well.

Battles are not the same as bondage. Engaging in battle is a designated privilege of free people. Bondage is bad; battle is good. Bondage makes you a slave; battles make you a soldier. A renewal of the mind is required to accept that fighting a battle from a place of victory is good. In fact, it is a key to victory.

When you get saved and delivered, battles don't stop. In fact, in some ways, they only begin. In deliverance, God works for you, but in dominion, He works through you. King David knew this about his God, *"Blessed be the Lord my Rock, Who trains my hands for war, and my fingers for battle"* (Psalm 144:1). God does not deliver you from battles, but He trains you for them. Because of the cross, we don't fight for victory; we fight from victory to victory. Like it or not, we must fight. Israel finally entered the Promised Land, but they still had to fight to take and maintain possession of it.

I believe by means of this book you will be trained to reign victoriously in your personal life. We will dive into the story of Esther and see the simple yet powerful process that takes us from deliverance to dominion.

It's time to fight back.

# Introduction

## Thoughts to Share
*Use #fightbackbook #pastorvlad hashtags.*

God has anointed you to resist that which you are asking Him to remove.

We were created to worship; we also were called to warfare.

Bondage is bad; battle is good. Bondage makes you a slave; battle makes you a soldier. Bondage happens in Egypt; battles take place in the promised land.

In deliverance, God works for you, but in dominion, He works through you.

God delivers us from demons but not from battles.

*Chapter 1*

# Battles That Didn't Start with You

I met Iveta for the first time in London while preaching at a youth conference called *Stay Lit* in 2019. She flew from Lithuania to meet my wife and me before deciding to come to our internship program later that year. Her testimony of deliverance and then walking in dominion has been a blessing to many people.

At the age of seven, her father was murdered. That's when she started to ask life's big question: "Who is God?" She remembers exactly when she learned what death is and that death can take a person you love. As a child, you never think about dying.

She remembers the moment during her father's funeral when the spirit of fear entered her. She was completely consumed by fear - afraid to die, afraid of the future and afraid of the unknown. Iveta started questioning righteousness, wondering if there was any justice in the world. She told her mom that one day she was going to get revenge and kill her father's murderer. She was consumed with hatred.

From that young age, her depression became very severe. She couldn't deal with her emotions; life became overwhelming. Eventually, she started causing harm to her body, and she was a threat to her very own life. When Iveta became a teenager, she was put on antidepressants for the next eleven years. Deep inside her mind, she felt unexplainable darkness. Strangely, she could tell that it was demonic. She actually asked her mom if she needed deliverance. This wasn't normal! Her issue was that she couldn't control her thoughts or obsessions which were constantly OCD (Obsessive Compulsive Disorder). She could not distinguish between what was actually real and what were her own thoughts or imaginations. Prescription drugs helped her a little, but she still felt completely empty.

Iveta felt like a victim but also a survivor. Pride consumed her. She began investigating the mystical spirit world. The mediums and fortune-tellers that she saw on TV told her that she could change her own future. By knowing her future, she thought she could predict events, romantic relationships, her future family, and outcomes of various situations. Because her family had a history of so many tragic events, suicides, losses of loved ones, murders, and overdoses, she felt it was her job to end her family curses. She planned to do that through witchcraft and astrology. She knew that demons existed, but she reasoned that she was in the "safe zone" because she was only practicing white magic. She reasoned that her intentions were good. After all, she just wanted to help people.

Fast forward, she began hanging out with the wrong crowds. She began drinking, partying, using crystals, veganism, New Age practices, and reincarnation, thinking the entire time that she was being enlightened. To her, this seemed to be solving her family's curses. Although she was paying her debts to karma, she still felt empty, restless, and anxious.

# Fight Back

One day Iveta happened to watch the testimony of a prominent woman who had been in the New Age movement for more than thirty years. The lady had a very lucrative business based on the New Age movement. The woman shared her amazing testimony about how Jesus had graciously saved her. She closed her business, burned all her books, renounced her practices, and even refunded the money people paid for all the materials she had sold them. There was no way this woman was faking it! So Iveta contacted the woman, who then led her in a prayer of repentance and salvation. Her eyes were opened to the idolatry she was committing by worshiping demons. She started to question her friends about the things that she had done and the way she was living. She felt conviction and heaviness for her sins. She literally felt like an unclean prostitute.

Iveta started repenting for everything. She believed in her heart that she was wicked! Prideful! How blind she had been to the truth! For the first time in her life, she felt God's loving protection over her even though she knew she still had open doors in her life. She kept on partying and living in sin; her conscience had been so badly damaged. Everyone and everything around her said that it was all right to live that way. She was deceived. They told her that there was nothing wrong with this kind of lifestyle. But when she was baptized with the Holy Spirit, her eyes were opened again. God started revealing true spiritual realities to her. He revealed what His will was for her life. He did not take the fun away, but He helped her to realize that spiritual consequences come after every decision. He showed her what He was saving her from!

Around this time Iveta was tormented by sleep paralysis (a feeling of being totally unable to move at the onset of sleep or upon awakening) as never before. The enemy attacked her through areas that weren't healed yet. She did not know that God had given her dominion and authority to send the devil running. The first time God showed her what she could do to overcome was when her grandmother passed away. Unfortunately, she couldn't attend her grandmother's funeral and she felt an overwhelming sense of guilt just hanging over her. Iveta woke up the following night and felt as though her deceased grandmother was lying beside her. She looked at her grandmother and felt an overwhelming sense of pain and guilt consume her. Then a thought clicked in her head, "Why would a loving God make me go through all this again?" So she declared out loud, "If you're not from Jesus, leave!" As soon as she said that, the demon left, annoyed. It was then she realized that there is power in the name of Jesus. She felt like God wanted to teach her that she indeed carried His power and authority.

Slowly, she started to learn how to deal with demonic powers. Eventually, God led her to watch my sermons on YouTube and to other ministers like Derek Prince. She started noticing what things she needed to throw away and get rid of, which were most of the things in her house. God also showed her that she still carried a lot of hatred. He asked her to forgive her father's murderer. When she finally did let go and forgive him, she received her total deliverance from hatred. It felt as though that dark part of her left. Wow! What joy! The heavy weight she had been carrying for years was lifted. She was free. She realized that living God's way is the best way.

I mentioned in my book *Break Free* that the devil uses open doors to gain access to an individual. Those doors are the occult, accursed things, trauma, generational curses, etc. The apostle Paul warns us, *"Nor give place to the devil"* (Ephesians 4:27). With Iveta, as with many

# Fight Back

young people today, unforgiveness and bitterness open the door to inner torment. Every door can be closed through faith and repentance. Freedom can be received by renouncing the access that the enemy might have had. What learning to reign in life through Jesus Christ.

## Esau's Hatred Resulted in Amalek's Attack

Let us now meet Queen Esther and look at her story in the Old Testament of the Bible. Before Queen Esther's deliverance from her enemy, the king's assistant Haman had made an evil plot to destroy her and all the Jewish people. Why? Let's look at when this battle against the Jews actually started. It began way before Esther was born. The conflict actually began with her ancestors Jacob and Esau, and it continued throughout history. *"So Esau hated Jacob because of the blessing with which his father blessed him, and Esau said in his heart, 'The days of mourning for my father are at hand; then I will kill my brother Jacob'"* (Genesis 27:41). This hatred in Esau toward his brother was never resolved. The talk of murder in his heart wasn't dealt with. No, Esau didn't ever hurt Jacob nor did he murder him, but it burned deep in his heart to do so.

The hatred that was in Esau's heart goes through the bloodline to his grandson, Amalek, and even further. *"Now Timna was the concubine of Eliphaz, Esau's son, and she bore Amalek to Eliphaz. These were the sons of Adah, Esau's wife"* (Genesis 36:12). Amalek's nation, who were descendants of Esau, was the first nation to attack Israel after Moses led them out of Egypt some 500 years later.

# Battles That Didn't Start with You

The Israelites didn't pass through the territory of the Amalekites and they posed no threat to them, yet the Amalekites attacked from behind - unexpectedly, indirectly, viciously and arrogantly. *"Remember what Amalek did to you on the way as you were coming out of Egypt, how he met you on the way and attacked your rear ranks, all the stragglers at your rear, when you were tired and weary; and he did not fear God"* (Deuteronomy 25:17-18). The Israelites were tired and weary. The Amalekites attacked the weakest stragglers lagging behind all the others. It was their typical way of fighting; they were sneaky, cruel, and barbarous (1 Samuel 30:1).

As Joshua went to physically fight the attacking army, Moses went to fight in the spiritual realm on the top of a mountain because the Amalekites were not just a physical enemy but also a wicked spiritual foe. After the victory was won, the Lord told Moses to *"Write this for a memorial in the book and recount it in the hearing of Joshua, that I will utterly blot out the remembrance of Amalek from under heaven"* (Exodus 17:14). In fact, Moses said, *"Because the Lord has sworn: the Lord will have war with Amalek from generation to generation"* (Exodus 17:16). God has sworn that He will have war with Amalek in every following generation.

Right before entering the promised land forty years later, Moses reminded Joshua of the same assignment, *"Therefore it shall be, when the Lord your God has given you rest from your enemies all around, in the land which the Lord your God is giving you to possess as an inheritance, that you will blot out the remembrance of Amalek from under heaven. You shall not forget"* (Deuteronomy 25:19).

In other words, God was really serious about removing Amalek. I want you to see the connection between

15

what happens when hatred dwells in the heart and what hostile inner "self-talk" in the head does to a person. Both of them need to be repented of. We can contain it and never let it get out of hand as Cain did, who let bitter hatred turn into a murder. Yes, Esau managed his animosity but never ever got free from it. However, years later it reappeared and his descendants turned that bitter rage into warfare.

God never called us to manage sin but to repent from it. The main reason is that it can get passed on to our children. What Esau had in his heart, Amalek had in his blood. This shouldn't surprise us since blessings and curses are generational. Our God is generational, being the God of Abraham, Isaac, and Jacob. So is hate, lust, pride, and every sinful tendency; they extend from generation to generation. That's why Solomon said, *"Keep your heart with all diligence, for out of it spring the issues of life"* (Proverbs 4:23).

## Saul's First Assignment

Some years after the nation of Israel entered their promised land, they received their first king whose name was Saul. His first assignment from God was to attack the Amalek people and utterly destroy all that they possessed. God said, *"I will punish Amalek for what he did to Israel, how he ambushed him on the way when he came up from Egypt"* (1 Samuel 15:2). But King Saul didn't take that assignment seriously and only obeyed God halfway, which God considered to be a sin of disobedience. King Saul spared Agag, the king of the Amalekites, and the best of the sheep, oxen, and other good things. Saul and his troops were unwilling to destroy everything. Saul's disobedience led to the loss of his kingdom as a consequence.

# Battles That Didn't Start with You

The repercussion of this disobedience goes even further than the loss of his kingdom.

Saul allowed King Agag to live and apparently some of his descendants escaped. Generations later, Haman was born, a descendant of Agag's family. This man Haman, *"the son of Hammedatha the Agagite"* (Esther 3:1), threatened to annihilate all the Jews living in Persia. And guess whom God raised up to face this descendant of Agag? It was Queen Esther and her first cousin Mordecai who were the direct descendants of Kish, the father of King Saul (Esther 2.5-6). Since King Saul had failed to obey God's instructions to kill King Agag, God re-stages the event many years later in Persia. This anti-Semitism spirit of Amalek rears its ugly head in Haman, but the Holy Spirit fills another son of Kish (Mordecai) to bring completion to the cycle of attacks and to finally finish him off.

## King Saul Passed on Enemies

Esther was called to fight a battle that she didn't start! Her ancestor King Saul should have fought and won that battle. He was the one anointed and appointed to finish off Amalek, but he didn't. King Saul should have passed on victories, but instead, he gave enemies to the next generation. These enemies didn't just disappear; the next generation had to face them. Queen Esther fought them and won by the power of God, and she passed onto the next generations a festive holiday called Purim in memory of her great victory over the old enemy that Israel had for a very long time.

Some of the battles you are facing today did not start with you but with your parents and grandparents. Maybe through their disobedience and sinful living, you have

# Fight Back

poverty, bad habits, sinful tendencies, and illnesses that were passed on to you. You are not responsible for what is passed on to you, but you are responsible for how you deal with sin, weaknesses, and failures. Perhaps the previous generations did not know about God, or they willfully walked in disobedience to Him. Instead of passing on victories and giving you a headstart in life, they passed on defeats and enemies of anger, lust, and addiction. Remember, you have the anointing that rested on Esther to put an end to the cycle of habitual sin, chronic sickness, fears, premature death, divorce, and poverty. Do not complain and blame the previous generation.

Esther didn't blame Saul. She recognized that her enemy was planning to annihilate her people only because Saul did not destroy him years earlier. God had chosen her for such a time as this, to win battles that she didn't start. They were battles that previous generations had been fighting. She didn't just continue these battles; she ended them. She passed victory on to the generations that followed her. What a celebration! At last, Amalek was no more.

I am not suggesting you start doing an inventory of your family tree to find out what your relatives did wrong. But if you look around and see that many in your family are always sick, you are the "Esther" to exterminate the Amalek of sickness in your generation. If you notice every marriage ends in divorce, you are the "Mordecai" to finish the Amalek of divorce in your family. Perhaps fear, depression, and anxiety run in your family tree; you are raised for such a time as this to overcome these demons in your family lineage. Perhaps there is poverty and a constant shortage of finances for everyone you know in your immediate family. Take courage. Just because battles were passed onto you, it doesn't mean you have to simply tolerate them; you need to end these battles in victory.

If you had great parents who passed on to you great victories, you have a great start in life. Don't mess it up by getting yourself involved in things that don't please God, because just as curses can be broken, blessings can be lost as well. If it feels like everything you touch turns to gold, take heed, and don't get proud; you are probably repeating generational blessings. You still have a role to play in choosing to walk in a way that keeps you in that blessing.

But if you didn't get the luxury of having victories passed on to you, the poor example that your parents gave you is not worthy to imitate. Remember, you are without an excuse. Parents decide your history, but your own choices decide your destiny. Choices are more powerful than statistics. If you surrender yourself to God and surround yourself with the right people, you will not become a statistic but a testimony of God's goodness. Esther had bad things passed on to her, but with the help of God and His people, she not only experienced deliverance but walked in dominion. Esther is your role model, demonstrating that your life doesn't have to be defined by what was handed down to you.

# Fight Back

## Thoughts to Share

*Use #fightbackbook #pastorvlad hashtags.*

Disobedience of one generation becomes defeat for the next, just as the sacrifice of one generation becomes the foundation for the next.

You are not responsible for what is passed on to you; you are responsible for how you react to it.

Parents decide your history, but your choices decide your destiny.

## Chapter 2

# Authority Trumps Access

Bob Hagen leads our prison ministry at the Hungry Generation. The Lord uses him to reach inmates with the gospel. He also travels to do missions overseas. But there was a time when Bob was a spiritual prisoner himself. He grew up a shy, introverted kid. During his childhood, his father studied metaphysics, the occult, and other related material. As a young child, he took much interest in his father's books which planted destructive seeds for his later life.

When the sixties came around, he chose to identify with the psychedelic subculture and started using marijuana and LSD. Suddenly, this shy introverted kid began to speak out boldly.

Bob would sometimes go into a catatonic or unconscious state for hours at a time. He met his friend Sam while in one of those catatonic states. Soon Sam introduced him to an organization known as the Brotherhood of Eternal Love, which was an association of hippies who were affiliated with an East Indian guru who taught self-realization. The "brothers" began to teach him. Eventually, they had him drive alone to a remote place in the mountains and take a massive amount of LSD. While under the influence, he was convinced that he had seen God.

This continued until narcotics officers began to investigate this organization and proceeded to arrest people. At

# Fight Back

this time Bob moved to Oregon and obtained a job in a mental hospital. While reading more books from his father's library, he found a book based on ancient teachings of Jewish mysticism which he studied at great lengths.

Bob felt like a weak and frightened man, who in an act of desperation had attempted to overcome his shyness and fears by placing himself in dangerous situations, both spiritually and physically. He had no real joy and was constantly restless.

During the fall of 1973, Bob went to visit his close friend who happened to be a Hindu priest and lived with his family in the Fiji Islands. The part of the island in which they resided was mostly Hindu. He taught Bob the rituals and ceremonies connected with this religion. One of the rituals was a "fire-walking" ceremony where people would walk barefoot over a bed of hot coals. Bob was there seven days before the lighting of the fire, and he intended to be a part of the ceremony. He practiced yoga and meditation constantly and convinced them that he was sincere about his search for enlightenment. While worshipping in the small temple, a variety of strange supernatural phenomenon's happened. Hindu spirits would take over people's bodies, and they would begin to act ape-like or display certain characteristics of their different gods, while others would fall in and out of trances.

Thousands of people gathered for the fire ceremony. Many even came from other countries. The fire-walkers all gathered at a lagoon, wetting their ritual garments in the water in order to prevent them from catching on fire. The priests would then approach every fire-walker and pierce their bodies with 6-inch metal needles. They were poked in various places - some through the cheeks and some through their sides, legs, arms, and neck. The strangest thing of all was that no blood appeared whatsoever! When it was Bob's turn, the priest took a long needle and pierced it through his neck so that the ends stuck out from both sides, but he felt no pain. Everyone chanted and walked through the fire, including Bob, without getting severely burnt.

Afterward, he left for New Zealand. Everything became worse day by day. Instead of becoming free, fulfilled, and happy as the priests promised, Bob began to experience real deep depression. He decided to throw himself into Scientology for the next 4 years, hoping to find some ease of mind there. He even became a licensed minister but found no comfort and no hope. He felt that he was actually further away from God than at any other time that he could remember. One night Bob called out to God and begged Him to help him. On a whim, he decided to fly back to visit his friend in Fiji thinking that maybe he left God there.

Upon arriving and staying there for a while, he realized nothing brought him peace - not even the deep insights of his Hindu friend. Bob, sick with a high fever, returned to the United States. The depression and confusion he had felt lasted for several years as he continued to search for answers. Nothing helped him. Not even all the spiritual books that he had ever read brought him the truth. He was desperately searching for God.

Some years later after he had returned to the States, he met Helen. They were dating at the time when she came to visit him for a Thanksgiving dinner. Bob was in the kitchen carving the turkey, and when he returned to the living room, he found Helen lying prostrate on the ground weeping. She told him that Jesus had just appeared to her.

# Fight Back

God then spoke clearly in his heart and told Bob that He wanted him to take care of Helen for the rest of his life. Bob and Helen were married, and she had the strength and wisdom to ground him in his faith with God. God used Helen to draw Bob closer to Himself and anchor him in faith. They both committed their lives to God in 1984, but the spiritual war inside of Bob continued until 1992. Before his deliverance, he felt really uneasy around the church and the body of Christ and battled with doubt. One day, a pastor from the Philippines told him he was in need of deliverance. It was on another Thanksgiving night when the pastor prayed over Bob. The next thing Bob knew, he was writhing on the ground restrained by 5 men. He realized he was chanting the same Hindu prayers he had chanted in the Hindu temple so long ago. Bob was finally delivered that night! He felt freedom as never before! The depression he had battled for so long left him and soon he started witnessing freely to people. There was a change even in his character with a complete sense of peace and joy.

He and his wife became a part of the Hungry Generation Church, faithfully serving alongside our team. Eventually, he started going to prisons, ministering to people there, as well as doing international mission trips. The anointing of the Holy Spirit would fall strongly on Bob. Whereas before he was afraid of speaking in public, that fear was completely lifted off and taken away. Often he sees remarkable deliverances, healings, and miracles during his outreaches and they continue to this day. The Holy Spirit revealed to Bob that to walk in victory requires drawing himself closer to Jesus constantly with discipline and devotion.

Seeing Bob every weekend at church reminds me that Jesus didn't come to just deliver us but to empower us to win in life. Unlike so many people who go from deliverance to deliverance, Bob went from freedom to fighting. Yes, sin opened the door to demons, but Jesus became his door to destiny. For twenty years now since his deliverance, he is walking in his destiny.

The enemy of our soul looks for open doors to enter through so that he can bring harm and torment. For Bob, drugs and the occult became the access key that the devil used to gain entrance into his life. Generational curses as we mentioned in the first chapter can give permission to the enemy to invade a person's life. The practice of sin, addiction, occult, unforgiveness, idolatry, accursed things, etc. are other open doors that give the devil access to a person's life. The devil may gain entry through the occult, abuse, accursed things, generational curses and willful sin, but there is something that is stronger. It can overturn his access. It trumps his access. It's called authority.

## Haman Had Access to the Palace

Haman had access to the place where Esther lived. Esther's house was his workplace. Haman worked in her palace, free and clear. In fact, he was promoted and advanced in that palace. His position was above all the other princes who were there with him. All the servants bowed and paid homage to Haman (Esther 3:1-2). In the palace where Haman worked, Queen Esther lived. But access did not give him ownership of that palace. He worked there, but he did not reside there.

As Christians, we must understand that through sin we give access to the devil. This access allows him to operate in our personal lives. Sin gives access but not ownership. Sin gives the devil a key to our house but it doesn't make our house his dwelling. Haman, who went to the palace to plot evil, returned daily to his own residence. The palace was not his home; it was Queen Esther's home. Even though he had access because of his position in the palace, the one matter he miscalculated was the authority that someone else had who lived there. Esther was the queen; he was simply a prince. Esther was married to Haman's boss. Esther had something much greater than just access to the palace; she had authority that comes with being married to the king.

A true born-again Christian can be oppressed by the devil if and when he gives access to the enemy, but he can't be possessed by the devil. This means Satan does not own the person, he doesn't possess that person. In *Break Free,* I devoted a whole chapter about the access the enemy can have in a person's life. This is an excerpt:

*When a Christian is delivered from demons or curses, it does not mean that those spirits had been living in his spirit. The Holy Spirit occupies the spirit of the believer, but demons can harass, torment, and oppress the soul of the believer. The Holy Spirit possesses the believer, meaning He owns him. Demonic spirits seek to oppress the Christian by controlling a part of his life. Being tormented by demons does not mean that you are not saved. It does not mean that those spirits own you. Derek Prince, who is a powerful influence on my life in the area of deliverance, shared in one of his talks that the Greek word New Testament writers used for demonic possession is "demonized." He would explain that being demonized does not mean ownership, but partial control. It means that demons seek to control one area of your life. They cannot have possession or ownership of your spirit. How do you know which area demons control? Usually, it is in the areas where you are not in control because some demon is dominating that area of your soul. When you get delivered, you get the control back. During deliverance, that part of your soul gets released. Maybe you are thinking, darkness and light cannot abide together. It does not say that in the Bible. Some think that the Holy Spirit and an evil spirit cannot dwell in the same vessel. Really? Says who? The Scripture that we get this from says, "Do not be unequally yoked together with unbelievers. For what fellowship has righteousness with lawlessness? And what communion has light with darkness?" (2 Corinthians 6:14). This verse does not say light and darkness cannot coexist. It says they should not exist together. Paul is telling us the way things should be, not what they cannot be. If you think Christians cannot be demonized, let me tell you, I have heard stories of when both light and darkness operated in the same person. For some examples, there was a fallen pastor who once preached holiness while frequently visiting prostitutes; a newly saved believer who habitually returned to drug abuse and suicidal attempts of self-destruction; a Christian leader who influenced many for the Gospel's sake but ended up in jail for fraud and thievery. Paul stated in 2 Corinthians 6:14, "Do not be unequally yoked together with unbelievers," and then went on talking about how darkness and light should not have any fellowship together. If darkness and light cannot coexist, then Christians cannot date unbelievers. We know that this happens all of the time. It should not, but it does. The same thing happens with demonized Christians. They should not be under this demonic influence, but nowhere in the Bible does it say that this is not possible."*[3]

[3] Savchuk, Vladimir. "Children's Bread." *Break Free*, Vladimir Savchuk, 2018, pp. 66–68.

# Fight Back

I don't want to focus on the power of access the enemy may have but on the power of the authority that believers have. When talking about spiritual warfare, we can be in danger of glorifying the devil. It's true that when we give him the key code to our life through sin, he will take advantage of it. He will seek to kill, steal, and destroy. If he can't kill, he will seek to destroy. If he can't destroy, he will at least steal something. You can be sure he will bring havoc in our life. The access that Haman had to the palace was used to plot evil against Esther and her people. The devil will do the same to anyone who gives him the key to their life by sinning. He will operate in our lives to plot against our peace, joy and prosperity. That should warn us not to commit sin but to walk on the path of holiness.

But even if you have given the devil access into your life, whether through willful sin or through someone in your past, you must understand how powerful is the authority of King Jesus. He is the king with whom we have a relationship. He is our bridegroom. We, the church, are His bride. No matter what access you have given to the devil and how far he has gone in destroying your life, in Christ Jesus you have the authority to remove that access key and take your life back from his grip.

Remember Bob's testimony at the beginning of this chapter? The enemy really had a grip on his life. He gave that access to the devil. He didn't know any better at that time. However, Jesus is not only merciful but also powerful. Through the power of the Holy Spirit, that access was canceled. The enemy was defeated, and now Bob is bringing freedom to others. I am not in any way advocating the "pleasure" of living in sin or downplaying the damaging effects of giving the enemy access, but I am declaring that Jesus' power is greater than anything in this world. He is omnipotent. He has total power to reign over your enemy.

# Authority Trumps Access

I remember talking with John Ramirez who was a satanic warlock in New York City. He has a powerful testimony that you can watch on YouTube. He mentioned one incident when a lady came to ask him to cast a spell on another person. John usually would charge a large sum of money for this sort of work. But when he found out that his neighbor wanted to cast a spell on a Christian lady, he told her that he would do it for free. He passionately hated Christians. He tried to cast a spell on this Christian lady, who at that time was living in adultery, but his spell wouldn't work. Something was protecting her from his spell. This was the first time he realized that there is a greater power out there than the power of the devil. I don't know why in this situation, even though the lady was living in sin, the enemy didn't have full control over her. Usually, he is able to. But I was encouraged to know that as Christians, we have more power in Christ than we realize. Satan is not as powerful as he portrays himself to be. He is a deceitful liar! Even though he is real and powerful, the authority we have in Jesus is far greater than Satan's power.

## The Believer's Authority

*"And He said to them, 'I saw Satan fall like lightning from heaven. Behold, I give you the authority to trample on serpents and scorpions, and over all the power of the enemy, and nothing shall by any means hurt you'"* (Luke 10:18). Jesus gave authority to the disciples before he gave them power. The power of the Holy Spirit came later, but the authority was given right away. Power is like the gun of the police officer, but the authority is the badge. When you become a Christian, Jesus gives you the authority as well as the power of the Holy Spirit. You are like a policeman in the spiritual world. A police officer has a badge

that represents authority and a weapon which provides power to back up that authority. Criminals are afraid of officers because of the authority and the power they carry. When you recognize the fact that authority and power over the devil has already been given to you, the enemy panics. He is the criminal, you are the officer. You have the power of heaven backing you up.

Jesus has all the authority in heaven and on earth (Matthew 28:18). We were given authority over all the power of the enemy (Luke 10:18). This authority is given so that we can trample on the enemy. Esther used the authority she had because of her relationship with her king, to drive out her enemy and trample upon his plot. Christ gave His bride the authority and power to do the same: to end the cycle of generational sins; to drive out spirits of fear, heaviness, bondage, divination, and death; to trample upon snakes, scorpions, and python demons; to break down strongholds that the enemy has built. Authority is not for show, it's for warfare.

## Believe in Jesus, Not Tradition

Some people are afraid to walk in God-given authority because of traditional religious teaching. This teaching causes fear in the hearts of Christians. This teaching is not in the Bible, and it benefits the devil very much. Traditional teaching says that if you are going to embark on the work of spiritual warfare, there will be repercussions and negative consequences for doing deliverances. They say that accidents, depression, heaviness, and nightmares are the devil's way of fighting back for walking in authority. I have heard some people warn young believers to be careful with doing spiritual warfare due to a dreadful backlash that might occur. I know all this sounds spiritual, but it is not scriptural. Jesus declared, *"Behold I give you the authority to trample on serpents and scorpions and over all the power of the enemy, and nothing shall by any means hurt you"* (Luke 10:19). That is a promise of protection for those who will *"trample on serpents and scorpions."* Jesus didn't warn his disciples about a possible backlash or that some hidden sin can cause the enemy to come and attack them. The early followers of Jesus weren't perfect, yet they had authority. The only warning Jesus gave was to not rejoice in our victories due to our authority but to rejoice in our eternal salvation which is the foundation of that authority.

When I was a teenager, I believed in this tradition more than in Jesus' teaching. I remember that before any big youth meeting where we would expect a huge harvest of souls and prayer for deliverance, we would pray fervently to cover ourselves with the blood of Jesus against potential attacks of the devil. Our problem was that we sincerely *expected* the devil to hit us back because of what we were about to do. We even told our leaders that we are going to cause damage to the kingdom of darkness and the devil will not just sit there idly, he will fight back. We thought that after great revivals, great attacks would follow. We used the stories of Jesus' temptation after his baptism at the Jordan River and Elijah's battle with depression after attacking the prophets of Jezebel as our proof that the enemy would attack us afterward.

The interesting part is that what we expected is what happened. Sometimes before conferences, our people would get into bad accidents like flipping on the highway while driving to the event, or singers would get so sick that they would have to be admitted to the hospital, or after the events, our team would get physically sick. All of that confirmed to us that what we were saying was really true.

# Fight Back

All those things were repercussions by the devil for causing damage to his kingdom, so we thought. That's what we
believed, but it was totally contrary to what Jesus promised. He said that "*nothing by any means shall hurt you*"
if we trample on the enemy. Jesus' words clearly carry
more weight than traditional teaching on warfare. Ever
since then, we have been teaching and standing on what
Jesus promised us, and we have done more deliverances
in one weekend than we used to do in one entire year.

It's not that the enemy does not attack us, but we
carry an invisible shield of faith in the spiritual world that
quenches all fiery darts of the devil (Ephesians 6:16). If
our faith is in what Jesus promised us, then that faith becomes a shield in the realm of the spirit. And if the devil
decides to attack back in retribution, the shield of faith
will stop that attack. Now, this doesn't mean that bad
times won't happen to those who walk in authority. What
I am saying is that we must not be afraid to exercise the
authority of Jesus, expecting the devil to fire back and
cause us to get wounded by his shots.

Another misconception I would like to address is this
idea that if you pray for the deliverance of someone, demons can enter you if you are not walking with God. First
of all, if there is an open door of sin in your life, the devil
doesn't need to wait until you see someone being delivered to take advantage of the open door which your sin
has provided.

Secondly, if during deliverance demons are removed
from one person only to go to the next person in the room,
does the same thing happen during the repentance of sin?
Do sins go from a sinner at the altar repenting to some
believer in pew number two? What happens during healing? Does the illness that one person gets healed from go

to another quickly? That's not true! Scriptures don't support that concept.

Behind all this misconception is the enemy attempting to instill fear into God's people to keep them from walking in the authority they have in Christ. Being in God's will is the safest place on earth. Preaching the gospel, healing the sick, and casting out demons is what we all should be doing. That's where God's protection is and demons know that.

Now it's time for us to recognize God's authority and protection and act on it. Our God has a better protection plan than Geico which can save you fifteen percent or more on your insurance, but God's plan has full protection coverage paid by the blood of Jesus.

## Dealing with the Defeated Devil

We are fighting a defeated foe. Our enemy with all his demons has been cast out of heaven after he was defeated there. Revelation 12:7-12 says, *"...he was cast down to the earth and his angels were cast out with him...the accuser of the brethren has been cast down...and they overcame him by the blood of the Lamb and by the word of their testimony."* After the fall, God promised that the seed of the woman will crush the head of the serpent (Genesis 3:15).

Jesus faced the devil in the wilderness and defeated him there, but the ultimate blow was struck by Jesus when he died on the cross and triumphantly rose from the dead. This is one of the reasons why the eternal Son of God had to become a man—because it was the offspring of the woman who would crush Satan. Jesus, *"having disarmed principalities and powers, He made a public spectacle of them, triumphing over them in it"* (Colossians 2:15). But that's not all! The church has been given the authority to continue destroying the works of the devil on the earth. Each time the gospel is preached, the sick are healed, the oppressed are freed, another blow is dealt to the enemy. We are also promised that a day is coming when the devil will be bound and thrown into hell and then eventually into the lake of fire where he will spend eternity.

To walk in authority, we must understand our enemy's past, present, and future. Yes, he is deceitful, tactical, smart, and powerful. But he is also defeated and has been disarmed by Jesus Christ. That's why we do not fight for victory; we fight from the position of victory. In the famous passage about spiritual warfare, Paul says to put on *"the whole armor of God to withstand in the evil day and having done all, to stand"* (Ephesians 6:11, 13).

The goal of our spiritual armor is not to get the victory, but to stand in the victory that has already been won for us. Paul is writing to believers who are not trying to gain victory by wearing spiritual armor but are standing in the victory that is already theirs in Christ Jesus. Stand in the victory of Christ. Put on the armor of God so that you can stand on what Jesus has already won for you. The devil will be defeated again and again as we go from glory to glory, from victory to victory.

That's why Apostle Paul calls us more than conquerors (Romans 8:37). A conqueror has the victory after a battle. We maintain that position of victory because we have dominion over the enemy; therefore, we are more than conquerors. Jesus defeated the devil, and because we are connected to Him, we partake of that authority. Like Queen Esther who had the authority because of her relationship to her king, so we walk in boldness because the King of kings has all the authority and he is our Husband. Our authority and dominion is directly connected to our identity as children of God and the bride of Christ.

## The Parts the Devil Doesn't Control

When Jesus arrived at the land of the Gadarenes after overcoming the fierce storm on the sea, He was met by a demon-possessed man who had a legion of demons living in him that caused him to dwell among the tombs. The naked man exhibited such supernatural strength that no one could bind him. He was crying out and cutting himself with stones. This guy was as possessed as they come.

What I find interesting is that this demon-possessed man quickly approached Jesus. *"When he saw Jesus from afar, he ran and worshipped Him"* (Mark 5:5). Imagine that! He ran and worshipped Jesus even while possessed by demons.

You don't have to know much about demons to know that they never cause people to run toward Jesus to worship Him. Actually, they work to pull people away from God. Many people who have been delivered testify that demons made them feel a strong, compelling desire to run away from a church service or feel extreme discomfort around God's people. If you remember Bob's testimony at the beginning of this chapter, after his salvation he felt uneasy around the things of God. Demons work hard to pull people away from God and the church. However, this demonized man ran up to Jesus and worshipped Him.

So that tells me that in spite of the fact that the man had a multitude of demons in him, he still had the ability to choose to run to Jesus and to worship Him. That caused Jesus to turn His attention to this desperate human being and deliver him. Even though demons controlled so much of him, the part that they did not control proved to be more powerful than the parts that they did control. This man was not born again. He didn't have the indwelling of the Holy Spirit to help him. But his sheer human will, whatever was left of it, was more powerful than the in-dwelling demons. Although his human willpower couldn't get him delivered, it brought him to Someone who could deliver him.

If a man having a thousand demons can run to Jesus and worship him, my friend, so can you. Don't give de-mons more power than they actually have by believing the devil's lie that demons are stronger than your willpower. Even if you feel oppressed and some parts of your life are still controlled by the enemy, remember, the part of your life that the devil has no control over is your will.

It is much more powerful than the parts that he does dominate. So, run to Jesus and worship Him and watch what He will do.

## The Struggle is Real

Unlike the demon-possessed man who ran to Jesus to worship Him, you are a born-again, Spirit-filled child of God. *"...You have overcome them because He who is in you is greater than the one who is in the world"* (1 John 4:4).

Lazarus was a friend of Jesus. He became gravely sick and died. When he died, they bound him hand and foot with strips of cloth and wrapped his face with another cloth. Jesus came to the tomb, and after the stone was re-moved, He shouted, *"Lazarus, come forth!"* (John 11:43). Jesus' command brought him back to life. He was raised from the dead! This is a huge miracle! Wouldn't you agree? If someone is raised from the dead after ten minutes, it's a big deal.

If someone is raised after being dead for four days, that's probably the biggest miracle there is. It's a bigger deal to be raised from the dead than to be bound up with grave clothes?

Resurrection is much more important than the binding grave clothes. Everyone who saw Lazarus alive after being dead didn't focus on his grave clothes or on the fact that he struggled to come out of the grave because he was bound by them. They were so exceedingly happy and excited that he was alive. Jesus did it. He brought life to a dead man. My friend, when you were saved, that's what Jesus did as well. He didn't come to Earth to make bad people become good; Jesus came to make dead people come alive. A spiritual resurrection happened when you were saved. Heaven threw a party. Angels were ecstatic of the miracle of your new birth.

But like Lazarus, your spiritual resurrection probably came along with some binding grave clothes restricting your hands or feet. Maybe following your salvation you have quickly noticed that this amazing miracle of salvation did not remove certain bad habits, addictions or chains. *"And he who had died came out bound hand and foot with graveclothes, and his face was wrapped with a cloth. Jesus said to them, 'Loose him, and let him go'"* (John 11:44). From Jesus' perspective, Lazarus coming back to life was a big deal. But place yourself in Lazarus' shoes. It was difficult to get up while being bound hand and foot. All Lazarus could think about were the grave clothes. No one came to carry him out of the tomb. He had to hobble out of it alone, and may I add, with a struggle. How do I know that? Many times, I have preached an illustrated sermon about this event. I would bind a person on the stage, hand and foot and cover his face with duct tape. Then I would lay that person in a pup-tent on the stage. Afterward, I would shout for him to get up and walk out on the platform. The struggle is real. The person who is alive but bound has to desperately struggle to get out of his *tomb*. While everyone in the audience is celebrating him for being alive, that person doesn't feel he received much of a victory. It is hard to walk out of the grave while still bound.

That's why I am here to remind you that your spiritual resurrection is more important than your spiritual rags. Forgiveness of sin is a greater gift than freedom from bondage. You can go to heaven with some bondage, but you can't go to heaven without forgiveness of sin. The greatest miracle is not deliverance but salvation. That's why Jesus said, *"Nevertheless do not rejoice in this, that the spirits are subject to you, but rather rejoice because your names are written in heaven"* (Luke 10:20).

Your resurrection is more powerful than your rags. My friend, your spiritual authority is greater than any access the enemy might have over you. Don't let your grave clothes hold you back from walking out of the grave. Lazarus was commanded to walk out of the grave while he was still bound. Was it easy? No! But he did it.

It was while he was walking out that Jesus sent others to loose him from his grave clothes. Surround yourself with people who will help you deal with the grave clothes. Sometimes we wait for God to send someone to loose us before we walk out of our grave. No, it's you who must make the decision to abandon your *grave* of toxic relationships, places where you are tempted to fall back into old sins or mindsets that you have embraced which are not in line with God's Word.

## Authority Trumps Access

If you want God to send someone to remove your graveclothes, then get yourself out of your spiritual grave when Jesus calls. The spiritual grave is where dead people live. A spiritual grave is a place where spiritually dead people hang out. It's those TV shows that dead people watch; those evil websites that dead people go on. A grave is a place for the dead.

You have more power in Jesus right now than you probably feel. You are stronger than you think. The same power that raised Jesus from the dead lives in you. With that power, you can drive out demons and be loosed from whatever chains that the enemy has put on you.

# Fight Back

## Thoughts to Share
*Use #fightbackbook #pastorvlad hashtags.*

Authority of the believer is greater than the access of the enemy.

Geico can save you fifteen percent or more on your insurance, but God offers full protection coverage paid by the blood of Jesus.

The goal of our spiritual armor is not to get the victory, but to stand in the victory that has already been won for us.

The part of your life that the devil has no control over is way more powerful than the parts that he does.

Every conqueror gets the victory after a battle. But, we have victory before the battle.

Don't let your binding cloths hold you back from walking out of the grave.

If you want God to send someone to remove your grave-clothes, then get yourself out the grave.

*Chapter 3*

# Our Weapons

Paulius was born and raised in a Roman Catholic household in a small city in Lithuania. As a young adult, he realized he did not want to spend the rest of his life in his hometown, so he studied hard in hopes of moving to one of the bigger cities to attend a university. He had the opportunity to study art and culture, meet new people, and travel to different countries. He and his new friends started partying, drinking, doing heavy drugs almost every night, and living immorally. Paulius didn't even realize how everything was getting out of hand, and he started slowly spiraling downward so much that he started losing himself. He fell into a bottomless pit of depression. He felt like he had everything he could ever want, yet he was so miserable and empty.

Sometime later one of his friends introduced him to demonic spirituality and meditation as a means to end his depression. Paulius started going to a yoga course that practiced "kundalini" meditation. Everyone who attended these courses seemed to be happy, and he wanted to try anything that would add more to his life. They taught him that he was his own teacher, and he should strive for enlightenment. Soon he was having out-of-body experiences, and he radically began searching the dark world for the truth. For the next two years of his search for truth, Paulius gained access to the New Age Eastern Mysticism, Hinduism, Shamanism, astrology, psychics, crystals, psychedelics, and anything else that you could ever imagine. He went to India to meditate with monks. He denied his body with constant fasting for days at a time. He was heavily influenced by all of these religions. While he tried to detach himself from this world, he still remained unhappy, never satisfied, never at peace, and his depression would come and go like a rollercoaster ride.

At one point Paulius brought himself to an almost near-death experience doing a 30-day juice fast, hoping to become more enlightened, but it only opened his eyes to how depleted he was spiritually, emotionally, and physically, nearly becoming mentally ill. He lay in bed recovering for weeks, and somehow in his room, he came across a diary of a Christian man. This book from cover to cover spoke about a powerful prayer: "Lord Jesus Christ have mercy on me." Time stopped as he repeated this prayer over and over again in his heart. Like never before there was a supernatural peace that enveloped him and he just wept. He couldn't stop praying, weeping, and asking God for forgiveness. Within the next 5 minutes, it was as though the cloud of darkness and depression that had followed him all his life left the room. For the first time, he felt God's tangible presence, perfect love, and an invitation to a new life. It made him realize just how wrong and undeserving he was.

Paulius didn't know anything about church other than the one he was raised in, nor did he know of a Christian community. He was in his room praying that same prayer day after day. During the next three months, the Lord showed him all his sins and their consequences. *"God's goodness leads us to repentance"* (Romans 2:4). He repented, and the demons that had been manifesting in his old life left him. Even though he didn't understand what was going on during these visitations, the Lord always brought him sublime peace. God gradually began opening doors and brought other born-again believers into his life. He joined a homegroup and received the baptism of the Holy Spirit. Deliverance was a process for him while God taught him how to walk in freedom.

Later on, Paulius came to the Hungry Generation internship program in Pasco, Washington, where he learned how to walk in victory and bring hope and salvation to others. Today, he is sharing the message of Jesus Christ with others in Europe, seeing them saved, healed, and delivered.

My friend Paulius was supernaturally delivered on his own by calling on the name of Jesus and praying in repentance. He is not the only one, but many others have also experienced what I call "self-deliverance."

Self-deliverance is the freedom you experience by yourself without anyone praying for you. Whether someone prays for you or you pray to God on your own, you must understand that the power is not in us but in God.

## The Spiritual World is Operated in Spiritual Ways

Spiritual warfare is fought with spiritual weapons. When Esther heard of the plot of Haman against the Jewish people, her first reaction was to fast and pray. Politically she was very well connected. Esther had powerful friends. She had a high position in the nation. I am sure she was very wealthy. She was resourceful. But her first act wasn't physical or political but spiritual. She asked everyone to fast on her behalf as she began to fast and pray. *"Then Esther told them to reply to Mordecai: 'Go, gather all the Jews who are present in Shushan, and fast for me; neither eat nor drink for three days, night or day. My maids and I will fast likewise. And so I will go to the*

*king, which is against the law; and if I perish, I perish!'"*
(Esther 4:14).

Queen Esther understood that behind Haman's plot were spiritual forces which could not be defeated by natural means. Esther didn't rely on her political connections first but on her spiritual connections. By fasting, all the spiritual forces controlling Haman were subdued, and a way was made for Esther to see victory in the natural realm.

If your problem is physical, it can be treated physically, but if the roots of that problem are spiritual, they have to be treated spiritually! If sickness is only physical, medicine can cure it; but if spiritual forces are behind it, medicine will be ineffective to cure it. We see this evidenced in Jesus' healing ministry, where in most cases He healed a sick person by casting out a demon. Physical problems at times may have deep spiritual roots. Those roots can be removed only by spiritual means. Esther discerned that an attack on her people was spiritual in nature; therefore, it would have to be fought first within the spiritual realm by prayer and fasting.

It's a huge mistake to deal with problems only in the natural realm when you have total access to spiritual weapons. As Christians, we are spiritual people and must act as such. The world we live in is more spiritual than we realize. Whether we want to admit it or not, we are always in spiritual warfare. We must engage in spiritual warfare by using spiritual weapons and walking with our spiritual armor on. Once we see victory in the spiritual realm, it will be easier to secure that victory in the natural domain. Esther went to the king for a solution only after she had fasted for three days. Time was of the essence, but she knew that without fasting, all her attempts in the palace would be futile. Spiritual warfare is fought in spiritual ways.

## The Weapon of Prayer

Prayer is a weapon to use in your spiritual warfare, but warfare is also needed during your prayer. In the chapter concerning spiritual warfare in the Bible, Paul said, *"Praying always with all prayer and supplication in the Spirit, being watchful to this end with all persever-ance and supplication for all the saints"* (Ephesians 6:18).

Prayer is a weapon, but it's also a battlefield. Fasting together with prayer was the weapon that Esther used to claim victory in the spiritual world. This weapon belongs to every Christian. Prayer "in the name of Jesus" has dynamic power in the spiritual realm. While casting out demons, I have often heard demons screaming how much they hate prayer and how prayer burns their kingdom. Prayer can bring deliverance. *"Then they cried out to the Lord in their trouble, and He delivered them out of their distresses"* (Psalm 107:6).

Some experience deliverance by going through a prayer line, others through a personal prayer life. By "prayer line" I mean when a minister prays for you; "prayer life" is when you pray for yourself on your own. Don't underestimate the power of your own spiritual weapon of prayer. Prayer mixed with humility, faith, and a deep cry unto God can do wonders in the spiritual world.

## Take Battle to a Spiritual Realm

Recently, I watched a video on YouTube of an eagle fighting a snake in midair. The eagle doesn't fight on the ground. It would not stand a chance with a snake. Snakes dominate the ground, but eagles dominate the air. The eagle took the snake into the sky and flipped it in the air, and that changed everything. Understand, snakes have no defense, no balance, and no power to strike in the air. On the ground, snakes are powerful and deadly, but in the air, they are weak, useless, and vulnerable. Your enemy is the snake; you are the eagle. Take your battle into the prayer zone, and he becomes defeated. Don't fight the enemy in his comfort zone; change the battleground like the eagle did, and let God bring you victory through prayer. Spiritual warfare is won in spiritual ways.

In the first recorded battle with the Amalekites, Joshua went to fight them physically, but Moses went up the mountain to fight them spiritually. *"And so it was, when Moses held up his hand, that Israel prevailed; and when he let down his hand, Amalek prevailed"* (Exodus 17:11).

Esther now followed this pattern in her conquest. She took the battle into the spiritual realm, and there she claimed the victory through fasting and prayer. She wasn't alone even as Joshua wasn't alone. Moses supported Joshua and all the Jews supported Esther in fasting.

## Prayerless Christians are Powerless Christians

Your enemy is spiritual but so are your weapons. Your enemy is deadly but so are your weapons. Your weapon is prayer. Peter, a disciple of Jesus, failed to use this weapon in his time of warfare. *"And the Lord said, 'Simon, Simon! Indeed, Satan has asked for you, that he may sift you as wheat. But I have prayed for you, that your faith should not fail; and when you have returned to Me, strengthen your brethren'"* (Luke 22:31-32). I find it interesting that this time Jesus refers to Peter by his old name Simon, the name Jesus had changed three years earlier (John 1:42-43). During the last supper, Jesus warned Peter that Satan had asked for him, but Jesus prayed for Peter. Not long afterward, in the Garden of Gethsemane, Jesus invites Peter to watch and pray with Him lest Peter fall into temptation. But Peter opted to prayerlessness, failing to use his spiritual weapon, and the enemy took the upper hand that night.

Prayerful Christians are powerful Christians. Prayerless Christians are powerless Christians. Prayer is a must because of the spiritual warfare that is constantly taking place in the unseen spiritual realm. If we fail to pray, we will stray back into our old patterns. Satan has the advantage over spiritually sleeping saints; he can sift them. Saints, it's time to wake up from your spiritual slumber and rise up in your spiritual authority. Do not treat prayer as your last resort but as the first response to every challenge that comes your way. Take your battles into the spiritual realm by prayer.

## The Weapon of Fasting

I want to highlight the power that is released through fasting. It's one of the weapons that Queen Esther utilized. Everyone of importance in the Bible practiced fasting: Moses, David, Elijah, Esther, Daniel, Anna, Paul, and Jesus, just to name a few. When Jesus taught on fasting, He said, *"When you fast"* not "if you fast." He assumed that we all would fast.

We were created to practice fasting. Think about it: if you sleep eight hours every night, then you are sleeping one-third of your lifetime. If you live about seventy-five years, that's twenty-five years of sleeping or 9,125 days.

# Fight Back

When you sleep, you are fasting and that's why the morning meal is called "breakfast" – it's when you break your fast.

Spiritual fasting is simply abstaining from food for spiritual reasons.

Fasting is the Biblical way to humble ourselves (Psalms 35:13; 69:10). Fasting helps us to overcome the calamities of life. For example, Ezra fasted for protection (Ezra 8:21-28). King Jehoshaphat fasted when the confederate armies of the Canaanites and Syrians invaded Israel (2 Chronicles 20:3).

Fasting also renews our hunger for God. When we fast, we gain our hunger back for the presence of God.

Another benefit of fasting is that it empowers us to fulfill God's calling on our life. Most of the people in the Old Testament fasted in a crisis. We should fast not only because of problems but also for a purpose. Anna fasted constantly for the coming of the redemption of Israel (Luke 2:37). Don't wait for problems to arise before fasting, but fast during problems. This is a great way to humble ourselves before God. Fasting should be a normal lifestyle.

One more reason to fast is for spiritual conquest.

*"Do not fear, Daniel, for from the first day that you set your heart to understand, and to humble yourself before your God, your words were heard; and I have come because of your words. But the prince of the kingdom of Persia withstood me twenty-one days; and behold, Michael, one of the chief princes, came to help me, for I had been left alone there with the kings of Persia"* (Daniel 10:12-13).

# Our Weapons

Daniel set his mind to humble himself before God through fasting. God dispatched an angel the moment Daniel set his heart to humble himself, but there was a serious conflict in the spiritual realm. Spiritual forces that dominate physical kingdoms and territories did not want him to receive his answer to prayer. But Daniel did not give up. God dispatched more angels and finally, the answer to Daniel's prayer came, twenty-one days later. Most of us are not fighting spiritual warfare on the level of national importance, but the very same weapons that great men of God used in the Bible are available to us as well. It's a matter of humbling ourselves before God in fasting. Whether you're seeking deliverance or wanting to walk in victory every day, develop a lifestyle of fasting. Fasting doesn't move God; it just moves us into His spiritual realm.

When I was bound by pornography, I humbled myself before God in fasting. God extended his grace to me and gave me freedom. Today, together with our Hungry Generation Church, we fast for three days every month as a lifestyle because we have a calling to fulfill, calamities to overcome, spiritual enemies to conquer and our personal connection to God to maintain. When you understand that the unseen world around us is spiritual, prayer becomes absolutely vital. When you come to the realization that there is a spiritual conflict going on constantly, fasting must become a regular habit. The spiritual enemy is always seeking ways to *"steal, kill or destroy"* your God-given joy in life (John 10:10). Fasting and prayer are vital weapons you must use to acquire victories. Instead of just dealing with the symptoms of problems, use these powerful tools to remove the root of spiritual issues and conflicts. Don't just deal with the symptoms; kill the roots.

# Fight Back

## The Power of the Name Jesus

Another powerful spiritual weapon is the "Name of Jesus." *"The name of the Lord is a mighty strong tower; the righteous man runs to and finds safety"* (Proverbs 18:10). Not only is the Lord's name a mighty tower of defense, but it's also like our spiritual password in prayer. Jesus instructed His followers to pray to the Father in "His name" (John 16:23).

In our church sometimes, our team leaders or volunteers use my name to get things done. For example, they can go to the church coffee shop and say, "Vlad said to get coffee" and the barista in the coffee shop will fill whatever they request because it would be like me asking. I have heard people say, we get further ahead getting things done when we use your name because people have respect and honor for you. Maybe, that's why Jesus said to come to the Father in His name, as though it were Jesus doing the asking. There is power released when you pray in Jesus' name.

We are saved by His name, *"for there is no other name under heaven given among men by which we must be saved"* (Acts 4:12). We are also baptized into His name (Acts 2:38). Miracles, signs and wonders are done in His mighty name (Acts 4:17).

When young David was fighting against Goliath, he boasted of coming against the giant, not with physical weapons, but with the name of his God. *"You come to me with a sword, with a spear, and with a javelin. But I come to you in the name of the Lord of hosts, the God of the armies of Israel, whom you have defied"* (1 Samuel 17:45). Young David knew that the name of the Lord is a mighty spiritual weapon in the spiritual realm. The dark spiritual world knows the power and authority of Jesus' name and it trembles. *"In my name,"* Jesus said, *"they will cast out demons and speak in new tongues"* (Mark 16:17). All that dynamic spiritual authority is in the name of our Lord Jesus Christ. *"Anyone who has faith in Me will do what I have been doing. He will do even greater things than these. I [Jesus] will do whatever you ask in My name, and I will do it to glorify the Father"* (John 14:12, 13). His name is a powerful weapon because it represents all that Jesus accomplished both in the natural realm here on earth as well as in the spiritual world. When you declare "the name of Jesus" with faith, it's as though Jesus himself were healing the sick, casting out demons and raising the dead. *"God has highly exalted Him and given Him the name which is above every name, that at the name of Jesus every knee should bow"* (Philippians 2:9).

One of my first experiences with the power of declaring Jesus' name came when I was a youth pastor around 20 years of age. A young man came to our youth group, and during the time of worship, he fell to the floor. There were church elders present at the meeting, so after worship, we surrounded him and started to pray. I was a bit confused, not knowing if it was a manifestation of the Holy Spirit or demons or maybe he just fainted. After five minutes into the prayer, violent demons started to manifest themselves through him. It was quite obvious that it wasn't the Holy Spirit or a physical issue that caused him to fall. We prayed for him for about an hour, shouting for the demon to come out of him. Something came out, but he was not fully delivered.

In our early days of ministry, our knowledge and experience about deliverance were very limited. So, we stopped praying and told him that we would fast and pray for him for the next three days, and then pray with him again a few days later. I was put in charge of taking him home. I was driving with him for about twenty minutes (for the Tri-Cities, a twenty-minute drive is far) in my dad's small red Toyota Corolla. He lived very far out of town in a place where there were no street lights and barely any phone reception. It was late at night, and there were only two of us in the car. He was much bigger physically than me. I opened my flip phone and saw there was no reception. It was spooky and honestly scary. Out of nowhere, he started to growl and act violently while I was driving the car down the middle of the road in total darkness with no phone reception. Now I realize that it was not smart for me to be driving him home alone.

With fear gripping me on every side, hanging on firmly to the steering wheel, I did what I knew I should do without the security of elders or pastors with me in the car. I started to shout with a demanding voice, "In the name of Jesus, I command you demon, let this man go." A few seconds later, he went back to his normal self and even the atmosphere in the car changed. He was big. It was dark and scary. I was all alone but it didn't matter; the name of Jesus is a mighty weapon. Please understand, Jesus' name is not a magical word.

The book of Acts tells us a story about the sons of a priest, Sceva, who tried to cast out demons by using the name of Jesus without personally knowing Jesus, and it backfired (Acts 19:11-20). Believing in the Lord and following Him empowers us to use that name with a mighty effect.

## The Power of the Blood

*"And they overcame him by the blood of the Lamb and by the word of their testimony"* (Revelation 12:11).

# Our Weapons

There is wonder-working power in the blood of the Lamb. Blood flows through the Bible even as it flows through our veins. If you cut the Bible, it will bleed; it is a bloody book. Blood is mentioned over three hundred times in the Old Testament and forty-three times in the New Testament.

We know from our school books that our body is composed of five to seven percent blood. Blood has seven functions in the body: it receives our waste like a trash can; it transfers oxygen throughout the body; it transports nutrients; it releases hormones; it maintains fluid balance; it circulates heat; and it fights microorganisms. God said, *"For the life of the flesh is in the blood"* (Leviticus 17:11). Even as physical blood in our body has many functions so does the blood of Jesus have power.

Typically, if you get blood on your shirt, it will leave a stain, but if you get the blood of Jesus on your heart, it will purify your heart. The blood of Jesus was shed *"for the remission of sins"* (Matthew 26:28); it gives life to those who consume it (John 6:53); it causes us to dwell in Christ and He in us (John 6:56); and it's the means by which Jesus purchased the church (Acts 20:28).

His blood redeems, justifies, saves, grants us forgiveness of sins and brings peace and reconciliation to God. His blood cleanses our conscience from dead works so that we can serve our holy God; *"How much more shall the blood of Christ...purge your conscience"* (Hebrews 9:14). It sanctifies us, and by Jesus' blood, we enter God's most holy presence with boldness: *"Therefore, brethren, having boldness to enter the Holiest by the blood of Jesus,"* (Hebrews 10:19).

# Fight Back

## Blood Speaks

The blood of Jesus Christ not only saves and sanctifies us, but it also speaks. Blood has a voice; it speaks. The writer of Hebrews said that we have come to Mount Zion and *"to Jesus the Mediator of the new covenant, and to the blood of sprinkling that speaks better things than that of Abel"* (Hebrews 12:24). The blood of Jesus speaks better things. When Cain killed his brother Abel, God came and asked, *"What have you done? The voice of your brother's blood cries out to Me from the ground"* (Genesis 4:10). God cursed Cain in response to the cry of his blood from the earth. The next verse says *"So now you are cursed from the earth"* (Genesis 4:11). God takes blood seriously and he can hear its voice. So, if Abel's blood cried out and a curse came upon Cain, how much more the blood of Jesus cries out better things, and it will bring you blessings instead. *"You have come...to the sprinkled blood that speaks a better word than the blood of Abel"* (Hebrews 12:24).

You might not feel powerful as a Christian, but remember that the blood of Jesus is your source of power. Jesus' blood is clean, perfect, precious, and powerful: *"...and the blood of Jesus Christ cleanses us from all sin"* (1 Peter 1:19; 1 John 1:7; Revelation 12:11). Even though Jesus is our Shepherd, He died as our sacrificial Lamb. Under the old covenant, the blood of sheep would only cover the sins of Israel, but under the new covenant of grace, the blood of the Lamb removes the stain of sin. John the Baptist said, *"Behold the Lamb of God who takes away the sin of the world"* (John 1:29). Praise God for the blood.

# Our Weapons

## Blood Brings Deliverance

We can see that the blood of Jesus has power. Your body uses white blood cells to fight the bacteria and viruses that invade you and make you sick. The blood in your body is a weapon against all sorts of enemies. And the same thing is said of the blood of Jesus. We overcome the devil through the blood. Just as our blood fights viruses and bacteria, the blood of Jesus overcomes demons, the devil, and spiritual darkness. This was beautifully portrayed when the people of Israel were getting ready to exit Egypt. They applied the blood of a lamb on the doorposts of their houses, and that night the death angel passed over their homes. Through the blood of an innocent lamb, they experienced the Passover. That was the night their ultimate deliverance became a reality. The nine plagues that brought tragic calamity for the Egyptians did not bring deliverance to the Jews, but this one act of shedding blood broke the grip of their enemy once and for all.

There is power in the blood. Believe in this. Declare the blood of Jesus over the entrance to your house, your family, your property, your neighborhood, your community, your place of employment, etc. Through your confession apply the blood of Jesus over the doorposts of your heart, mind, and soul.

Regularly take communion to remember the awesome power of the new covenant that you are in. I encourage the sick to take communion daily during their devotions. There is power in the blood of Christ. The devil gained access to humanity by what they ate; they ate the forbidden fruit. They ate themselves out of paradise. The same way we eat our way back into victory through eating. *Then Jesus said to them, "Most assuredly, I say to you, unless you eat the flesh of the Son of Man and drink His blood, you have no life in you. Whoever eats My flesh and drinks My blood has eternal life, and I will raise him up on the last day. For My flesh is food indeed, and My blood is drink indeed. He who eats My flesh and drinks My blood abides in Me, and I in him"* (John 6:53-56).

Eating of His flesh and drinking of His blood through communion brings life and invites His presence to abide in us, bringing us into a consistent awareness of Him. If you lack victory right now and feel like there is no life in you or feel as though you wandered out of your spiritual paradise, begin to take communion during your devotional time. Meditate on the Lord's death. Remember the new covenant that you are in.

One of the most difficult deliverances I witnessed was that of a girl who was possessed by a powerful demon due to a blood covenant that her parents created with the devil when she was a child. Our strongest ushers couldn't hold her down. Sometimes, curses brought on through a blood covenant with demons are the hardest to cast out. By the name of Jesus, she was delivered through the power of the Holy Spirit because Jesus' blood covenant is more powerful than any demon. When you take communion, you remind yourself of that covenant as well as activate all the benefits of that covenant to manifest in your life.

## Sword of the Spirit

In the USA the right to keep and bear arms is a fundamental right protected by the Second Amendment to the United States Constitution, part of the Bill of Rights. Though I don't own a gun, many of my friends do. Americans take guns very seriously. In fact, America is the number one country in the world with most gun owners. There are more guns in the USA than people. As journalist Christopher Ingraham from the Washington Post writes,

# Our Weapons

*"With an estimated 120.5 guns for every 100 residents, the firearm ownership rate in the United States is twice that of the next-highest nation, Yemen, with just 52.8 guns per 100 residents"*[4]. Warfare in the world has changed from who has the strongest soldiers to who has the best weapons. Out of all the spiritual armor that Paul mentioned in Ephesians chapter six, the sword is the only offensive piece of the armor that is used for the purpose of fighting. The rest of the pieces of armor are for our personal defense, for the purpose of standing in the victory given to us by Jesus. *"And take the helmet of salvation, and the sword of the Spirit, which is the word of God"* (Ephesians 6:17). This sword of the Spirit is the Word of God. It's not called the sword of Jesus nor the sword of the Father but of the Holy Spirit. That means that the Word of God is empowered by the Holy Spirit. The power of the Spirit is released by God's Word.

As we have mentioned before, the anointing of the Holy Spirit brings deliverance. You experience the same anointing that flows out of God's word as you quote it by faith. You can experience self-deliverance, as in the case of Paulius mentioned above. The Holy Spirit doesn't just operate through ministers, but you yourself can use His mighty Word to bring about deliverance and dominion. Every believer has access to this powerful weapon.

## Spiritual Stabbing

Victory over the enemy is possible by using the sword. Jesus modeled that for us in the wilderness. Jesus didn't

---

[4] Ingraham, Christopher. "Analysis | There Are More Guns Than People in the United States, According to a New Study of Global Firearm Ownership." *The Washington Post*, WP Company, 19 June 2018, www.washingtonpost.com/news/wonk/wp/2018/06/19/there-are-more-guns-than-people-in-the-united-states-according-to-a-new-study-of-global-firearm-ownership/.

use His own name or divine nature to cause the devil to be defeated. He used the Scriptures. He used the sword of God's Word. And this sword works every time, *"For the word of God is living and powerful, and sharper than any two-edged sword"* (Hebrews 4:12).

It's important to emphasize that Jesus spoke the Scriptures out loud against the devil. *"But He answered and said, 'It is written'"* (Matthew 4:4). Most of the devil's attacks will be in our mind, but our fight against these attacks has to be with our mouth. When Satan throws darts at you in the form of your thoughts or feelings, don't fight back with "thoughts." Open your mouth and speak out the Scriptures as Jesus did. The Word of God declared out of your mouth has the same power as the Word of God out of Jesus' mouth. Fighting demonic thoughts with human thoughts doesn't bring victory. Demonic attacks are fought with the sword which is God's Word spoken out of your mouth.

That's why God told Joshua, *"This Book of the Law shall not depart from your mouth but you shall meditate in it day and night, that you may observe to do according to all that is written in it. For then you will make your way prosperous, and then you will have good success"* (Joshua 1:8). Have you noticed that Joshua was commanded to let the Scriptures come out of his mouth so that they would reinforce his meditation? Your words lined up with God's Word redirect your personal meditation and thoughts. When Scriptures are spoken, you get the upper hand in the battle. God's promise for speaking the Word out of your mouth is that your thoughts will be filled with a meditation on God's Word and *"then you will make your way prosperous, and then you will have good success."*

# Our Weapons

Fight the spiritual enemy with the sword of the Holy Spirit by declaring God's word out loud. It might sound strange and it will even feel weird at first, but remember, your words are swords in the Spirit realm. They are affecting the devil even if you don't see it with your physical eyes. Every time you are speaking the Scripture you are stabbing Satan. That is what is happening in the spirit realm. After a while, the devil will flee from you as he did from Jesus.

## There was no Sword in the Hands of People

Many Christians depend entirely on their pastors to study the Bible and then teach it to them. While it's true that pastors and teachers are called to do that, it does not exempt us from taking the responsibility to have and use our own swords.

*"So it came about, on the day of battle, that there was neither sword nor spear found in the hand of any of the people who were with Saul and Jonathan. But they were found with Saul and Jonathan his son"* (1 Samuel 13:22).

I fear that we have a similar situation in the Church today. Saul and Jonathan were the only ones in Israel who had swords. Saul and Jonathan represent preachers who study and preach the Word. When the Philistine enemy conquered the Israelite people, they confiscated all the weapons the people had in order to prevent them from rising up in rebellion and set themselves free.

In most parts of the world today, it's not illegal to have a Bible, but the enemy fights with us over our personal time so that we don't stop to read, study, memorize, meditate on, confess and obey the Bible. Time is a precious commodity and God wants us to take a "time out" every

# Fight Back

day so He can talk to us.  Satan doesn't have a problem with you owning a Bible as long as you don't use it.  If a sword is not used, it's useless, and that's the same thing with your Bible.  If it sits on the shelf untouched and is not in your heart and mouth, it profits you nothing.

You are in a war.  It's time to pick up your weapon.  If you own a gun you probably go to the range to practice shooting at targets.  But just having a gun doesn't make you a sharpshooter. And so is it with the Bible. Just having a Bible app on your phone doesn't prepare and equip you to use the sword.

Start reading the Bible daily.  Matthew 6:11 says "*Give us this day our daily bread.*" Find a translation that is easy to read and understand.  If reading your Bible is difficult or inconvenient for you to do during the day, subscribe to a plan on a Bible app. Sneak a peek at the Word throughout the day.  God asked Joshua to "*meditate day and night,*" at least twice every day.

Listen to God's word regularly. "*Faith comes by hearing and hearing by the word of God*" (Romans 10:17). Reading is very important, but listening to God's word is equally important. Most Bible apps now offer you free audio versions of the Bible. Take advantage of listening to God's Word.

Begin to memorize Scripture verses on a regular basis. During spiritual attacks by the devil, the Holy Spirit can bring to your memory only the verses you have put into your "memory bank."  Therefore, make a dedicated effort to memorize verses.

Another good practice is meditating on the Scriptures. Unlike demonic meditations where folks empty their mind, we meditate by filling our mind with the Word of God.  Meditation is a time devoted to reflecting and

# Our Weapons

contemplating on what God wants to tell us. Don't just read tidbits of the Bible. Snack crackers, cookies, and diet soda do not nourish you. Take big portions of the Bible to observe in context what God wants to communicate.

Think about what you have read and seen and how you can apply the passage to your daily living. Find out what virtues you need to practice. The strength of your spiritual life is in exact proportion to how much God's Word occupies your heart and thoughts. Don't just read the Bible; think about it all day long.

Use the Word of God in your prayers. I like quoting the promises of God in my prayer time. That makes my prayers always line up with God's perfect will. Remember God said, *"My Word shall not return to Me void, but it shall accomplish what I please"* (Isaiah 55:11). He can't go against His word when you quote it in prayer.

Use the sword that's in your hand and expect results. Confess God's Word out loud. Speak His word into your situation. Declare His unchangeable promises to your problems. Sometimes you have to speak Scriptures to comfort your soul. Speak the opposite of your negative feelings. When the devil attacks you, speak God's Word against him.

Prior to meeting Lana, my number of texts would be around 700 per month. When I fell in love with Lana, the following month I sent over 9,000 SMS messages. Yes, that was a lot. It wasn't that I fell in love with texting; I was in love with a person who happened to live three and a half hours away from me. Texting was our way of communicating. I looked forward to getting messages from her every morning and returning texts to her as well. The Bible is full of God's texts to us. It contains over 31,173 verses. God "texted" them to us because He loves us. Being in God's Word is not only your spiritual weapon but also a way to express your love for hearing from Him.

## Don't Feed the Bird

*"Behold, a sower went out to sow. And as he sowed, some seed fell by the wayside; and the birds came and devoured them* (Matthew 13:3-4). In the parable about the sower, the key to all His parables, Jesus said that birds came and ate the seeds that fell on the wayside. Later on, He explained what that means: *"When anyone hears the word of the kingdom and does not understand it, then the wicked one comes and snatches away what was sown in his heart. This is he who received seed by the wayside"* (Matthew 13:19). The bird wants to eat the seed so that it won't produce a harvest. This wicked bird is the devil who wants to steal the word so that we don't get fed, encouraged, or empowered by it.

Satan is on a mission to take God's Word away from the believer. That's the only weapon the devil has as a defense mechanism for himself. He knows he can't win against the use of the Scriptures, so he fights us to make sure we don't understand, read, listen, memorize, meditate, or confess the Scriptures. He knows that otherwise, we would be spiritually healthy and fruitful in our endeavor to walk in spiritual dominion over him and his demons. He makes us "too busy," distracted, lazy, or disinterested in the Bible.

When you feed yourself, you will starve the bird. Sadly, most Christians have been feeding the bird by neglecting the word of God. Don't empower the enemy by not feeding yourself. Negligence results in weakness. When you deprive yourself of receiving nourishment from

# Our Weapons

the Scriptures, you are empowering your enemy. The bird gets fed while you starve.

The words by Mr. Boggs printed inside the cover of the New Testaments distributed by The Gideons International say,

*"God's word is God's gift to humanity. It reveals the mind of God, the state of man, the way of salvation, the doom of sinners, and the happiness of believers. We have to read it to be wise, believe it to be safe, and practice it to be holy. The Bible is light to direct you, food to support you, and comfort to cheer you on. It's the traveler's map, the pilgrim's staff, the pilot's compass, the soldier's sword, and the Christian's charter. It should fill the memory, rule the heart, and guide our feet. We should read it slowly, frequently, and prayerfully."[5]*

Esther used the weapon of fasting, but you and I have even greater and more powerful spiritual weapons to use which are mighty in God, such as fervent prayer and fasting, using the name of Jesus, knowing and declaring the Word of God, and claiming the blood of Jesus. Our victory is not in the arm of the flesh but in the armor of God.

---

[5] "An Inspiring Introduction To The Holy Book." *The Gideons International*, 18 May 2011, blog.gideons.org/2010/12/the-bible-contains-the-mind-of-god/.

# Fight Back

## Thoughts to Share
*Use #fightbackbook #pastorvlad hashtags.*

Spiritual warfare is fought with spiritual weapons.

Prayer is a weapon, but it's also a battlefield.

Some experience deliverance by going through a prayer line, others through personal prayer life.

Prayerful Christians are powerful Christians.
Prayerless Christians are powerless Christians.

Satan has the advantage over spiritually sleeping saints; he can sift them.

We fast because we have a calling to fulfill, calamities to overcome, spiritual enemies to conquer and our connection to God to maintain.

The blood of Jesus has a voice, and it's a weapon against forces of darkness.

The Holy Spirit can't bring to memory verses you didn't memorize.

## Chapter 4

# Royalty in Rags

Hiroo Onoda was a young Japanese soldier in World War II who had a unique story. He was one of the several Japanese soldiers who continued fighting on their former battleground in the Philippines, long after the war had ended in August 1945[6]. He took seriously the order from his commanding officer to never surrender because desertion of a military assignment came with the heavy price of punishment, shame and dishonor.

Every Japanese soldier was prepared to die in combat, but as an intelligence officer, he was instructed to conduct guerrilla warfare. The world first heard about him in 1950 when his fellow comrades came out of hiding and were returned to Japan. He was still holed up in a cave on the Philippine island of Lubang because he refused to disobey his commander's orders.

The Japanese military had sent many search parties and dropped leaflets, trying to convince him that the war was over, but he dismissed them as traps and enemy propaganda. While Onoda was on the Island, he fought with local residents and killed about 30 civilians, mistaking them for enemy soldiers.

Finally, the government sent his former commanding officer, who had given him the initial orders, to go to his hideout in the mountains and persuade him that the war

---

[6] McCurry, Justin. "Hiroo Onoda: Japanese Soldier Who Took Three Decades to Surrender, Dies." *The Guardian*, Guardian News and Media, 17 Jan. 2014, http://www.theguardian.com/world/2014/jan/17/hiroo-onoda-japanese-soldier-dies

was really over, 29 years later. When he flew back to Japan he was greeted as a hero. He was also pardoned by the Philippine president for killing non-combatant citizens.

Onoda wept uncontrollably in relief as he finally laid down his rifle. Hiroo Onoda died at the age of 91 in 2014, having opened a series of survival schools throughout Japan after his return[7].

This powerfully illustrates how knowing the truth will set us free. That's why the apostle Paul teaches, *"...but be transformed by the renewing of your mind"* (Romans 12:2). Our life is changed by the renewing of our mind. God already did all the work, but if our mind is not renewed with the truth, we live in hiding and bondage.

From the story of Esther, we have learned so far that the authority of the believer trumps the access of the enemy. Some of the battles did not start with us, but they will end with us. Also, spiritual war is fought with spiritual weapons like prayer and fasting. Following fasting, Esther put on her royal robes to come into the presence of the king. *"Now it happened on the third day that Esther put on her royal robes and stood in the inner court of the king's palace, across from the king's house, while the king sat on his royal throne in the royal house, facing the entrance of the house"* (Esther 5:1).

## A Spiritual Shift Leads
## to a Shift in the Mind

Victory in the spiritual realm must be preceded by a shift in the mind. Fighting spiritually requires one to dress up mentally. Following her time of fasting, Esther dressed

---

[7] "Japan WW2 Soldier Who Refused to Surrender Hiroo Onoda Dies." *BBC News*, BBC, 17 Jan. 2014, www.bbc.com/news/world-asia-25772192.

up in royal garments. Esther's personal dress code reflected her royal position in the palace, not her actual condition. She was dressed up in regal garments, not rags. Esther's dress code is symbolic of the believer's mindset. Our way of thinking has to reflect our position in Christ, not our current crisis.

Therefore, we have to come dressed up in the royalty of God's promises, not dressed in the worn-out rags of our problems. Our current situation should not decide our dress code. Esther was going through hell, but she didn't dress in sackcloth and ashes when approaching the king. She refused to let her situation choose her wardrobe. This is one of the mistakes we make as believers; we let our warfare choose our wardrobe. We let what we are going through dominate our mind, will, and emotions toward God and ourselves. We expect God to change our lives before we change our attitude and the way we think. But it doesn't work that way. Romans 12:2 says that our life is transformed after our mind is changed.

## What You Wear, You Represent

Esther didn't wait for the king to solve the impending problem she faced before she dressed up as his queen. Renewing of the mind requires a refusal to conform to the world. *"And do not be conformed to this world, but be transformed by the renewing of your mind"* (Romans 12:2). Notice that *"do not be conformed"* comes before *"be transformed."* It's so easy to conform to your mental "dress code," to the menacing world, crisis, sickness, poverty and defeat. Stop allowing your problems to choose your dress code.

When I travel to speak, often the host church gives me a gift of their best merchandise, a t-shirt. I accept the gift, but to be honest, I don't wear everything I get. Some merchandise I keep, and some I give away. I think the same applies to life. When you experience poverty or bankruptcy, the financial distress will give you a t-shirt, a mindset to put on. When you go through defeat in some area of your life, that defeat will give you a t-shirt to wear. The devil offers you a t-shirt to wear because he wants to bind your thoughts at the level of your recent failures. But you don't have to wear everything you receive. Remember, Esther, teaches us that we don't need to wear ashes and rags just because we are under attack. We don't have to constantly think at the level of our problem. How we feel is not that important; what really matters is how we think. We are what we think, not what we feel.

One of the reasons people want me to wear their merchandise is to represent their ministry to others. That's totally cool. I love doing that if the t-shirt is of good quality or if I really want to represent their ministry to my friends. Honestly, that's why the devil wants you to "wear" the problem that's filling your mind. He is not just interested in you to have sickness in your body only but also to have that sickness in your thoughts. He wants you to let your sickness become your identity. He wants you to represent to others his work of destruction by letting your mind be subject to your dilemma. It's you who must choose what to wear. You represent what you wear, and what you wear represents you.

## The First Key to Renewing Your Mind
### - *Don't Conform* –

Esther didn't give pleasure to Haman by dressing as an orphan. Formerly she had been an orphan, but now she was the queen. She didn't wear tattered rags, but she put on royal garments. The evil plot of the enemy had not yet been reversed, but Esther didn't wait for that to happen before dressing up in royal garments. The victory had already been won in the spiritual realm for her, so she represented that victory by dressing accordingly. Renewing of the mind comes before the transformation of life. At times we put off changing our way of thinking until God changes our circumstances. In fact, we even blame our circumstances for our state of mind. We say things like, "When my life gets better, then my disposition will get better."

Esther didn't wait for Haman to die before she dressed up like a queen. Nor should you. Your life will not change unless you change your way of thinking. The enemy, Haman, will not be defeated if you don't get dressed up as royalty. Your emotional outlook must reflect who you are, not what you are going through. Our thoughts must be filled with the promises of God, not with the problems of life. Remember, we are ambassadors of Christ (2 Corinthians 5:20), not representatives of crisis. Scripture says, *"humble yourself in the sight of the Lord, and He will lift you up"* (James 4:10).

That means we must stop humbling or subjecting ourselves to life's situations. The first key to renewing your mind is refusal to conform to your situation. In other words, never let your situation or problems decide your "dress code."

## The Second Key to Renewing Your Mind
### - *Fill Your Mind* –

The second key to renewing the mind is to fill our minds with the truth of God. Esther put on royal garments. She already had them in her closet, but now she wore them. Jesus said, "*If you hold to My teachings, you are really My disciples. Then you shall know the truth and the truth will set you free*" (John 8:32). He spoke to His disciples who already believed in Him. Knowing the truth is directed to believers. It's not being surrounded with the presence of truth that sets us free. Instead, it's the knowledge and application of the truth that brings freedom.

Truth is like soap; it only works when applied. If you have a truckload of soap but do not apply it on your skin, it will be useless. Simply knowing the truth according to the Bible does not automatically change your life. You must ultimately know and practice that truth, which by its very nature starts to bring freedom into your mind.

Truth is more than just facts; it is what God says about Himself and us. Facts change; truth does not. Truth is unchangeable. A man called Muhammad believed that he was a prophet of truth. Buddha felt that he was a seeker after truth. But Jesus said, "*I am the Truth*" (John 14:6). Truth can be found only in Jesus. The more we personally know Jesus, the more truth we learn about ourselves and the more freedom will occupy our minds. "*But put on the Lord Jesus Christ, and make no provision for the flesh*" (Romans 13:14). We as Christians not only trust in Jesus but "we put on Jesus." We do this by identifying with Christ. Since we were joined to Him, we became one spirit with Him. "*But he who is joined to the Lord is one spirit with Him*" (1 Corinthians 6:17). When we are baptized, we are baptized into Christ's death, burial, and resurrection. Water baptism is for our identification with Jesus Christ. "*Therefore we were buried with Him through baptism...*" (Romans 6:3-11).

# Royalty in Rags

## Put on the Royal Garments

As Christians, we have the truth because we have Jesus, just as Esther owned royal garments in the palace. The key is to put on those royal garments. Royal garments are like the truth. Just having those garments is not enough; wearing them is what brings results. Maybe your problem is lingering, and there is a delay in the solution. As with Esther, even after fasting, everything seemed to remain the same. But things were actually getting worse for her; however, Esther didn't panic or fall into despair. She put on her royal attire. Don't forsake the truth of God's word about yourself just because your circumstances don't seem to be changing immediately or the symptoms of your sickness even return.

Prolonged problems tend to cause us to think as orphans. We dress like orphans. We talk as orphans. Yes, Esther had been an orphan, but she dressed up as royalty even though the immediate threat was still confronting her. It's easy to give in to our feelings and abandon our faith when things we had hoped for don't turn out as we expected. It's also easy to give up on the revelation of God's truth when the actual reality seems to contradict it.

I want to encourage you to dress up as royalty when you feel like an orphan. You're not an orphan; you are a child of God. Don't let your situation change your revelation; let your revelation transform your situation. Don't let reality change your mind, but renew your mind with truth, and your life will be transformed.

Dressed in majestic royal garments, Esther approached the king. The palace was her home, but it had been invaded by an enemy who had access. In fact, her palace had become a place of warfare and she showed up to combat properly dressed. In his writing, Paul tells us about the importance of proper dress code in spiritual warfare (Ephesians 6:10-20). *"Put on the whole armor of God, that you may be able to stand against the wiles of the devil"* (Ephesians 6:11).

Esther's dress code was royal garments; ours is the whole armor of God. As Esther put on those noble garments, even so, we are instructed to put on the armor of God which includes faith, righteousness, salvation, truth and peace. We are not required to produce it but are directed to wear it. This armor is God's provision to every believer. Every Christian has the armor of God, but not every Christian wears it. Armor doesn't work if it's not worn.

## It's Not About Having but Wearing

I have a 49cc Honda moped, which I use to get around town, go to work or visit family on warm days. Its top speed is 35--40 miles per hour. In my state, it's required by law to wear a helmet when riding a moped. At the time of writing this book, I live less than a minute's drive from the church where I work. Last summer while riding back and forth to work, I made excuses why I don't need to wear a helmet while riding my moped. I am embarrassed to admit that for a few weeks I was riding the moped without a helmet. It's not that I didn't have a helmet. In fact, I had three helmets. It's just that I didn't put one on. One time while driving back home on a wonderful sunny day, a police officer followed me home and he gave me a ticket.

I didn't get a ticket because I didn't have a helmet; I got a ticket because I wasn't wearing one. Of course, it's better to get a ticket than to get an accidental head injury. Since that time, I always put on my helmet every time I ride my moped. I wonder how many believers do the same with the whole armor of God. We have it; we just don't wear it. As a result of not wearing it, we aren't walking in the victory that Jesus bought with his precious blood.

We are getting spiritual tickets, spiritual attacks. We are unable to stand up to the wiles of the devil, unable to withstand the evil day, unable to quench all the fiery darts of the wicked one, and constantly being hurt and harassed by the enemy. Our problem is not that we don't have the armor of God; we're just not using it.

Don't just store God's armor in your head; you need to "dress" your mind and actions with it.

## The Helmet of Salvation Instead of the Hat of Condemnation

For example, we put on the helmet of salvation by believing that we are saved and by confessing it. We are saved by the grace of Jesus through faith. The gift of salvation makes us children of God. He prepares a place in heaven for us and enables the Holy Spirit to live in us.

Salvation is a helmet that we must wear. By living constantly aware of our salvation, we protect our minds from the attack of the devil. Believers have the helmet of salvation but often choose to wear the hat of condemnation. Their mind is filled with guilt and shame, living in constant fear of losing their salvation. But your salvation is in Jesus and it's secure.

Put salvation on your mind. Don't wear hats of guilt, shame and fear; put on salvation. Confess with your mouth that Jesus is your personal Savior. No one can snatch you out of His hand. Having salvation protects us from the wrath of God, but wearing salvation protects us from the attacks of the devil. Selah.

## From Rags to Righteousness

The same is true for righteousness. Our human righteousness is as filthy rags, but Jesus' righteousness is bulletproof (Isaiah 64:6). Righteousness is more than just forgiveness. It's right standing before God. *"For He has clothed me with garments of salvation and arrayed me in a robe of righteousness"* (Isaiah 61:10). Jesus became sin so that we can be made righteous. Jesus was not a sinner, but He became sin on the cross so that I will be righteous in Him. I am not righteous in myself. Jesus died on the cross taking upon Himself my sins so that I can live as a righteous person. This robe of righteousness is powerful protection from the condemnation of the devil.

If salvation protects the head, righteousness protects the heart. If our heart condemns us, we have something bigger than our heart which is the blood of Jesus. The cross is greater than our heart. That's why Jesus' righteousness protects the heart. Through righteousness, we are as bold as a lion (Proverbs 28:1), not easily shaken (Psalm 112:6), and get up after we fall (Proverbs 24:16). Blessed are those who thirst for righteousness (Matthew 5:6). God delivers the righteous man from all afflictions (Psalm 34:19). We reign in life through the gift of righteousness (Romans 5:17).

Every believer has this righteousness, but not every believer puts on His righteousness. This means that they aren't constantly aware of who they are in Christ. Most of us live with sin consciousness, not righteous consciousness. As a result, we get spiritual heart attacks. The devil attacks our hearts because we are not "wearing" right-eousness. It's time to take off your rags of self and put on His righteousness. Change your clothes and boldly go to the palace of the king arrayed in your royal robe of right-eousness. Believe that you are righteous. If you don't feel it, look to the cross. It's not about feeling it but believing it. Confess that you are righteous. Be constantly aware of your righteousness in Jesus Christ. That is your royal garment. That is your dress code for spiritual warfare.

## It's Not About Winning but Standing

It's vital to notice that spiritual armor is not for winning a battle but is used for standing firm in the victory.

*"Put on the whole armor of God, that you may be able to stand against the wiles of the devil"* (Ephesians 6:11).

Again, Paul says, *"Therefore take up the whole armor of God, that you may be able to withstand in the evil day, and having done all, to stand"* (Ephesians 6:13).

And again, *"Stand firm"* (Ephesians 6:14).

Your spiritual armor enables you to stand in the victory that Christ has already won. It enables you to firmly withstand the attacks and the fiery accusations of the wicked one, the devil. It's true that the Bible says *we do* wrestle against principalities, powers, rulers, and spiritual hosts, but we wrestle from a position of victory. We don't fight for victory; we fight from victory. The main purpose of the armor of God is not for fighting but to enable us to stand firmly in the victory of Christ. Just stand and do not move from your position of victory.

# Fight Back

## "The Evil Day" Happens to Good People

Spiritual armor is our royal dress code to help us stand in the "evil day." An evil day can happen to all good people. An evil day can come to righteous people. Esther had that evil day, yet she dressed up in her royal garments as a queen in her royal position in the palace. Everyone experiences an "evil day." It can begin with everything that can go wrong, does go wrong. You may feel over-whelmed. In those times you have to remember that the things happening around you are more spiritual than you realize. It might feel like you don't have the strength to fight back. But all you need to do is stand. Just stand! Dress up your mind, heart and feet with the reality of whom you are in Christ and then just stand.

Remember, if you put on the whole armor of God, it will be only an evil "day" for you, not evil days. That's a promise; an evil day will end and the next morning God renews His mercy. *"For His compassions never fail. They are new every morning; great is Your faithfulness"* (Lamentations 3:23). This verse has been a source of strength for me in the "evil day" of my life. The devil would whisper, "This evil day will not end; it will continue. You're a failure, a total loser, nothing ever works out in your life." I usually responded back to him, "You are a liar! This is your trick to use an evil day to make me into an evil person, but you were defeated on the cross. Even on this day, I will stand in my position and withstand your oppo-sition." I can't tell you how many times the next morning everything would be new and different. The evil day had come to an end. Period! God didn't give us spiritual armor to help us avoid an evil day but to help us avoid becoming evil people due to evil days in our life. The spiritual armor is given to us so that an evil day doesn't turn into an evil week or an evil month or an evil year or even an evil life.

# Royalty in Rags

The devil's strategy is to use the evil day to turn you into an evil person. But God gives you a solution: His armor. It doesn't prevent you from having the evil day, but it will protect you from becoming an evil person. It will limit how long that evil day lingers. When the evil day comes, don't panic.

Put on your royal robe.

By **faith** stand in your position of victory.

Confess your **salvation**; eliminate condemnation.

Proclaim Jesus' **righteousness** over you even when you don't feel like you're righteous.

Claim the **truth** of God's Word even when events contradict it

Declare the **peace** that passes understanding when you feel confused.

Speak **God's Word**, not your feelings.

You will be amazed at how that kind of attitude will change the spiritual climate of your evil day. The enemy will be pushed back. You will take back the ground from the enemy.

## Don't Fight People

It's important to notice that we don't put on God's armor to wrestle against flesh and blood, "for we do not wrestle against flesh and blood, but against principalities, against powers, against the rulers of the darkness of this age, against spiritual hosts of wickedness in heavenly places" (Ephesians 6:12). In other words, we are not at war with people. It's not possible to live victoriously in the spiritual realm while clashing with people in the flesh.

# Fight Back

That's why Paul reminds us that we don't wrestle against flesh and blood.

God anoints us for winning spiritual battles, not arguments with people. We are not called to squabble with people. The devil entices us to engage in battles that are not ours. Do not fight people. The wicked one tempts us to fight our brothers and sisters so that we forget to fight him. Don't waste your anointing on battles that God didn't call you to. To walk victoriously in the spiritual realm, we must stay focused and walk away from conflicts with people, no matter how enticing those battles may be.

## Put on Jesus Christ

Let's read this account again and slowly.

*"Now it happened on the third day that Esther put on her royal robes and stood in the inner court of the king's palace, across from the king's house, while the king sat on his royal throne in the royal house, facing the entrance of the house. So it was, when the king saw Queen Esther standing in the court, that she found favor in his sight, and the king held out to Esther the golden scepter that was in his hand. Then Esther went near and touched the top of the scepter"* (Esther 5:1-2).

Esther had fasted. She put on her royal robes and then stood in the inner court. When the king saw her standing all dressed up, the Bible says that she found favor in his sight, and he held out the golden scepter. She touched the top of that scepter. She knew that she had not been summoned into the royal court. There was a protocol that if you came uninvited into the king's presence, you would die unless he extended his scepter to you.

# Royalty in Rags

When by faith we put on the Lord Jesus Christ - His righteousness, salvation, truth, peace and use His word - not only do we stand in the position of victory, but we also attract God's favor on us. God no longer sees us but He sees His Son, Jesus. We become the fragrance of Christ to God Himself. That releases God's favor on our life. Esther desperately needed a solution for her problem, and when the king extended his scepter, everything started to change from that point on. Breakthrough!

We also must put on royal garments, not only to stand against the enemy but also to stand in God's awesome presence. Although it's true that we can come to God the way we are, I want to encourage you to come into God's presence dressed up. Don't come wearing spiritual pajamas if you want to obtain His divine favor. The pajamas I refer to are like when we murmur and complain, telling God our doubts and fears, quoting Him facts, leaving our spiritual armor at home, and coming into His presence clothed in spiritual rags. Yes, God is loving indeed and will accept us, but we are talking here about His grace and favor. He gives grace and favor to those who are dressed in regal garments.

## Jacob Wore His Brother's Clothes

When the patriarch Jacob wanted to receive a blessing from his father Isaac, he came dressed up like his older brother. He didn't need to do that if he simply wanted to have a conversation with his dad. But Jacob wanted his father's favor and special blessing. He knew that he couldn't come dressed up like himself because the blessing really belonged to the firstborn of the family, his brother Esau. It's something like that with us and God. Jesus is the firstborn; He is the righteous one who deserves blessing and favor.

# Fight Back

We are God's children and can always come into His presence. But if we want to receive something special from our Father, we are instructed to ask in Jesus' name.

*"If you ask anything in My name, I will do it"* (John 14:14).

*"You did not choose Me, but I chose you and appointed you that you should go and bear fruit, and that your fruit should remain, that whatever you ask the Father in My name He may give you"* (John 15:16).

We put on Jesus' righteousness as Jacob put on his brother's garments. The only difference is that Jesus gives us these garments, whereas Jacob had to steal them. And neither is our father God blind as Isaac was. God extends favor and mercy to us because we come in Jesus' name, dressed up like Jesus, even smelling like Jesus since we are the fragrance of Christ to God.

It's very important that you understand the meaning of this. If you feel like certain problems are lingering and some evil spirits are still operating in your life, maybe curses are hovering over you. Take your battle into the spiritual realm. Put on your royal robes. Don't wait for everything to be resolved in the physical realm first before you begin to think and act like a champion. Put on your spiritual armor and think, talk and act like a victor, not a victim. God will extend to you His favor. And you will see the glorious manifestation of victory.

# Royalty in Rags

## Thoughts to Share
*Use #fightbackbook #pastorvlad hashtags.*

Don't let your problems determine your mental dress code.

Our minds must reflect who we are, not what we are going through.

Our thoughts must be filled with the promises of God, not with the problems of life.

Truth is like soap; it only works when applied.

Truth is more than facts. Facts change; truth is stable.

If you don't let your situation change your revelation, then your revelation will transform your situation.

Every Christian has the armor of God, but not every Christian wears it. Armor doesn't work if it's not worn.

Having salvation protects us from the wrath of God, but wearing salvation protects us from the attacks of the devil.

God's armor doesn't prevent an "evil day," but it protects us from becoming an evil person.

God anoints us for winning spiritual battles, not arguments with people.

Don't waste your anointing on battles that God didn't call you to.

*Chapter 5*

# Warfare in the Wilderness

Vera was a young woman who couldn't maintain a healthy friendship. She would go from one relationship to the next, all the time struggling to keep it alive. This lifestyle troubled her and saddened her family greatly. During this time she battled with explicit sexual dreams. Whenever she would watch a movie or overhear a dirty conversation, that same night she would experience filthy, impure dreams. This distressed her extremely!

She would wake up crying because she had no control over her dreams. She felt so dirty, impure, and alone. Throughout the day, Vera would completely shut down, isolate herself and fall into depression. She knew this was not at all normal; she had to do something about it. Then she remembered a testimony of a woman from church named Gladys, who also used to struggle with sexual dreams which were a result of having a demonic "spirit-husband." Before she was actually delivered, Vera did whatever she could to break every curse and pray all the prayers she could think of to bind the demons but without results.

She made a decision to go through the prayer line at church. Vera started to pray against any possible mystical "spirit-husband" relationship and quickly her body went weak. She had to struggle for every breath she took. She wasn't sure what was happening, but she trusted that God would set her free. Demonic powers began to manifest as she fell to the floor weeping. Even though she couldn't control her body, her mind was alert and fighting.

I was finally able to get to her and cast the demon out in Jesus' name. After the demon was expelled, Vera experienced a supernatural peace that came over her mind and body. The unbearable weight was gone; she felt as light as a feather, and she overflowed with joy. She went home and slept throughout the entire night without any horrible dreams.

But this was just the beginning of a few more battles because she had to learn how to use the authority that Jesus had given her. If those dreams bothered her in the night again, her mentor taught her to rebuke the dreams in Jesus' name. It was through a process of deliverance that Vera learned to fight with the help of her mentor right there by her side. When Vera developed a deeper relationship with God, she found true deliverance.

It has been four years now, and Vera is happily married to her husband with two beautiful children. She and her family are devoted to serving the Lord with their Hungry Generation church community.

Let's go back to the story of Esther to learn more about warfare. We know so far that Esther had a wicked enemy who had access to her palace, but she was the one who had the authority. First of all, she fought her physical enemy by fasting spiritually. After a period of fasting, she dressed up in her royal garments and went to the king.

What strikes me the most is that Esther didn't immediately ask for deliverance for her people, the Jews. When the king asked her what was her wish, what was her request, her response was unexpected: *"If it pleases the*

# Fight Back

*king, let the king and Haman come today to the banquet that I have prepared for him"* (Esther 5:4).

A banquet?

Really, Esther?

The Jewish people are about to die. You are about to die. You don't have time for feasting. The king already asked you, Esther, what do you want? Just tell him why you came and about Haman's evil plot. But Esther doesn't do that. Her request is for the king to come to a banquet.

## The Tale of Two Queens

First, let's rewind this story to the beginning of the book of *Esther*. Before Esther came on the scene, there was another queen whose name was Vashti. During weeks of feasting hosted by the king, Esther's predecessor Vashti decided to have a feast of her own for the women. During that time, the king ordered his wife Vashti to come to his banquet hall so that he could show her off to his colleagues. But she refused to come! She was busy at her own banquet with the women. Her husband was furious and the next thing you know, she lost her crown. Her refusal to come into his presence as she was ordered was enough reason for the king to remove her crown. She didn't cheat on him nor plot to kill him. In fact, she was serving women at another banquet hall. Just that refusal to come when she was commanded cost Vashti her crown. Now, compare the two queens.

> Vashti was commanded to come and see the king, but she refused. Esther was not invited to go see the king, yet she went.

> Vashti led women to a feast. Esther led a nation to a fast.

# Warfare in the Wilderness

Vashti prepared a banquet for women. Esther prepared a banquet for the king.

Vashti loved the palace. Esther loved the king.

Vashti lost her crown. Esther won and saved a nation.

## Ministry to the Lord Comes First

This is a reminder for me as God's servant to not let my ministry to people become a distraction from my personal ministry to the Lord. I don't want to act like Queen Vashti who considered banquets for people to be more important than coming into the presence of her king. Don't get me wrong. People do matter to me because they are the reason why Jesus died on the cross.

But in my prayer time, I reflect often on this verse, *"It is not desirable that we should leave the word of God and serve tables"* (Acts 6:2). The twelve apostles did not ignore the needs of people. They just realized that with all this busyness that demanded so much of their time, they were ignoring essential quality time with the Lord. Therefore, they decided to delegate the work to good leaders so that they could be free to *"give [themselves] continually to prayer and to the ministry of the word"* (Acts 6:4). The results of this decision to spend maximum time in God's presence were astonishing. *"Then the word of God spread, and the number of the disciples multiplied greatly in Jerusalem, and a great many of the priests were obedient to the faith"* (Acts 6:7). Notice the word *"then."* After their decision to give themselves continually to prayer, not just occasionally, God opened to them a greater dimension of ministry. God's word spread more, disciples (not just decisions) multiplied, and influential people became followers of Jesus.

# Fight Back

Whenever I become overwhelmed in my ministry or even with the cares of my life, I do what the apostles did and take inventory of my devotional life to see if I am neglecting my quality time with the Lord.

## One Thing is Needed

Many Christians burn out because they neglect to minister to the Lord. Like Queen Vashti, they lose their crown. In other words, they neglect their authority, anointing, hunger and sensitivity to the Lord because they are too busy to come into His presence when He summons them. If you live in the United States, you may be summoned to serve on a jury. You take those summons very seriously; they can not be treated as junk mail. The same should be true with God. He summons us into His presence daily. Sadly, some believers treat a summons to jury duty more seriously than God's summons to prayer and to reading His word.

The consequence of not spending much quality time with God is obvious. It is similar to what Martha experienced when Jesus said, *"Martha, Martha, you are worried and troubled about many things"* (Luke 10:41). She heard those words, *"worried"* and *"troubled about many things"* while preparing food for her best friend Jesus and His disciples. How could this be? Martha was not doing anything sinful. She was just busy doing what was urgent but neglected the most important thing, which was spending precious time with Jesus. *"But one thing is needed, and Mary has chosen that good part, which will not be taken away from her"* (Luke 10:42).

*One thing* is needed, not many things.

# Warfare in the Wilderness

*One thing* is to spend time at Jesus' feet and hear His word.

*One thing* is what Martha wasn't doing.

*One thing* is what Mary chose to do.

*One thing* is a good thing.

When we neglect the "*one thing,*" we get trapped into worry, anxiety, fussing and many other problems. Like Martha, we start to blame others and even blame God. We fall into self-pity. We live in constant stress. But the secret to overcoming all of these problems is to stay in prayer, in God's presence, and in God's Word. Then our prayer time will turn into a delightful time with Jesus instead of just an ordinary routine discipline. Feed yourself with God's Word; don't just read it. Spend much time with the Lord! Then all your works for God will flow out of your personal, intimate relationship with Him, including His anointing, authority, favor and success.

## Getting Back Your First Love

Let's come back to Vashti who refused to come when the king commanded. Her disobedience cost her the crown. Most likely, Vashti became a concubine when she lost her position as queen. She probably remained at the palace but had no relationship with the king. But one thing of which we are sure, she was no longer the queen.

I find similar warnings in the book of Revelation to the church of Ephesus. This church did not lack good works, labor, patience, or perseverance. Jesus commented that they have "*labored for My name's sake and have not become weary*" (Revelation 2:3). They worked hard for the Lord but neglected the Lord Himself. In the next verse, Jesus gives a loving rebuke, "*Nevertheless I*

*have this against you, that you have left your first love"*
(Revelation 2:4). Unlike Vashti, who never got a second
chance, the church of Ephesus got another chance to do it
right.

Jesus outlines the process of coming back to your first
love. *"Remember therefore from where you have fallen;
repent and do the first works"* (Revelation 2:5).

Remember, repent, and repeat the first works. These
are three simple steps to coming back to your "first love."
It all starts with remembering and reflecting on how
things used to be at first. Then you must turn to repentance, a change of mind that results in a change of direction. After repentance, you choose to be zealous again in
doing the first works. This is how you regain your first love
for Jesus.

If you don't make these adjustments to come to the
Lord, the consequence follows. *"Or else I will come to you
quickly and remove your lampstand from its place—unless you repent"* (Revelation 2:5). The consequence was
that the lampstand would be removed from its place. The
church of Ephesus was warned that their lampstand
would be removed. A lamp provides light in the dark. It's
as though Jesus was saying, you will lose your influence
in the dark spiritual world. You will no longer have His
spiritual authority nor walk in His anointing unless you
reflect, repent and return.

## Showing up Uninvited

So we see what happened when Vashti refused to go
to the king when she was ordered to do so. Now, let's con-
sider Esther. She went to the king even though she had
not been invited. For thirty days her husband, the king,

had not invited her to be with him. *"Yet I myself have not been called to go in unto the king these thirty days"* (Esther 4:11). That must have been hard on Esther. On top of all that, she was dealing with the overwhelming crisis of a potential wipeout of her people, the Jews, so she worked up the courage to approach him without an invitation.

I get encouragement from Esther's example that occasionally when I don't feel like coming to the Lord, I still know that I should.

At times we may lack the desire to go to the Lord because of the weight of problems, stress at work, pressure in ministry, or crisis in finances, but we are never in Esther's position, where we feel uninvited.

God is always ready to receive us and He lovingly welcomes us into His presence.

## Spiritual Hunger Comes by Eating

Sometimes we just don't feel the Holy Spirit leading us to seek the Lord's face. The devil might be filling our head with lies that God doesn't care about us anymore. Sometimes we hit a dry season during which we feel absolutely no desire to pray, fast, or read the Bible. Often, that lonely season involves spiritual warfare. Whenever you don't feel like going to King Jesus is when you need to go to Him the most, in spite of your feelings. When you lose your hunger for God, you must force-feed yourself with His Word, even if you don't feel like doing it. A spiritual appetite grows by eating. A spiritual hunger follows spiritual feeding. Push yourself to eat whenever you want to have a greater hunger for God. Physical hunger comes by not eating, but spiritual hunger follows after eating. The more you enjoy fellowship with God, the more you crave Him.

# Fight Back

If you are losing your hunger for God, force-feed your-self until hunger kicks in. When you don't feel the Holy Spirit moving in your life, feed yourself on the Scriptures until you do. That's Him talking to you. Don't submit to your feelings when you're in the spiritual wilderness or under spiritual attack. Feelings can't be trusted, especially when you are facing challenges. Feelings must not dictate your behavior. I know it's easier to write about this than it is to live it. Doing what is right, even when we are not feel-ing close to God, develops spiritual maturity. Our faith flourishes when feelings fail. Don't attach your faith to feelings; connect your faith to Jesus. He never fails! Go to the King when you feel "uninvited," unmotivated, dis-couraged, sad and defeated. Just take the initiative to lin-ger with Him and enjoy His friendship. His presence is your solution!

## God Rewards Those Who Seek Him

I want to take this feeling of "not invited" a little fur-ther. In my younger years, it was hard for me to go to the King when I didn't feel His presence for a while. It was discouraging, but I have learned a few things that have changed my perspective. One of them is to feed myself even though I don't feel anything. When I can't control my feelings, I am still responsible for what I am feeding my-self.

The second truth I learned is that God promised to reward those who fervently seek Him, not who only find Him: *"But without faith it is impossible to please Him, for he who comes to God must believe that He is, and that He is a rewarder of those who diligently seek Him"* (He-brews 11:6). We don't seek God because He is lost. He is always near us because His Spirit lives within us. We go to prayer not to find God but to be with Him. With that said, there are seasons in life where it seems and feels like His manifest presence is gone.

During these seasons you must understand that God is building up your faith since Jesus is the author and perfecter of your faith. *"Let us lay aside every weight and sin which so easily ensnare us...looking unto Jesus, the author and finisher of our faith"* (Hebrews 12:1-2). Without faith, it is impossible to please God, and this faith gets stronger as your feelings get weaker. You are forced to rely only on God's Word, not on your feelings or experiences. In seasons of your spiritual wilderness, only faith can help you come closer to God. If you live by your feelings, you will feel distant from God. When you go to God's throne in spite of your negative feelings, you are building your faith. Here is a little fuel for your faith: *"God is a rewarder of those who diligently seek him"* (Hebrews 11:6). I find it encouraging that He is not a rewarder of those who feel or experience Him but of those who do their best to seek Him.

King David was called *"a man after His own heart"* (1 Samuel 13:14). God didn't say that David had His heart; he was simply after it. David was in constant pursuit of God. In reading the Psalms that he wrote, we see his heart's journey into the presence of God. At times he would complain that he didn't feel God, yet he was still seeking after Him. God likes that. He wants us to pursue Him, even when we don't feel like it.

In fact, not only does God love that we pursue Him, but He also rewards us. This truth has been the source of my encouragement. I don't submit to my feelings, but I let my faith grow by going to God no matter what's happening in my life.

# Fight Back

You might be under a spiritual attack or in a spiritual wilderness today. The enemy is working extra hard to keep you away from the presence of God Almighty, but don't yield to his temptation. Don't pamper your feelings. Don't talk about them. By faith believe that God is with you, and he will reward you when you pursue Him. Esther went to the king uninvited; nonetheless, she received her reward of mercy and grace. And so will you whenever you go to God's throne of grace in spite of your feelings (Hebrews 4:16).

## In Between Deliverance and Dominion

Israel left Egypt, which was their place of deliverance, but the promised land they were heading for was their place of dominion. In between Egypt and the promised land was a dry desert. People, on their journey to exercise dominion in their promised land, once they have experienced deliverance from Egypt, usually travel through a spiritual wilderness. The period between deliverance and dominion is usually marked by a miserable wilderness.

Elijah went through a wilderness as well as the apostle Paul (1 Kings 19:1-9; Galatians 1:17-18). Even our Lord Jesus *"was led into the wilderness to be tempted of the devil"* (Matthew 4:1) after being filled with the Holy Spirit. The wilderness experience is a tough time in which we endure spiritual afflictions. Often it's a time when temptation intensifies; there might be spiritual attacks on our soul. This is a time that may also involve a spiritual drought when we feel disconnected from God. A spiritual wilderness is not a sign that we are in sin although sometimes it feels like that. Instead of looking for God, we tend to look for some sin that can be blamed for our current experience.

# Warfare in the Wilderness

Not only can we overcome our wilderness experiences, but also we can shorten them by the way we respond. Whenever we can't control what happens around us, we must not fret about it. Instead, we need to control the only thing we can control, which is our response. When we can't control our circumstances, we can control our confession, attitude and response. How we react in the spiritual wilderness will determine how long we will stay there. Israel's wilderness time was not supposed to be forty years, but it was extended only because of their reaction to potential problems in the promised land. "*According to the number of the days in which you spied out the land, forty days, for each day you shall bear your guilt one year, namely forty years, and you shall know My rejection*" (Numbers 14:34). Complaining prolongs your spiritual wilderness; confessing God's Word shrinks it. Compare Jesus with Israel. His wilderness time lasted only forty days, not forty years. What did Jesus do in the wilderness? Well, He did not complain, He confessed God's Word.

We usually don't get to dominion right after deliverance without passing through a spiritual wilderness. We must learn to confess God's Word while in the wilderness in order to see our wilderness come to an end. After Jesus spoke the Word in the wilderness, that period of temptation ended, and He entered into ministry in the power of the Holy Spirit. "*Now when the devil had ended every temptation, he departed from Him until an opportune time. Then Jesus returned in the power of the Spirit to Galilee, and news of Him went out through all the surrounding region*" (Luke 4:13-14).

# Fight Back

## Silence is Not Absence

Back in the days when I was in school, every time the teacher gave us a test, there was silence. Before the test, the teacher would teach but during the test the teacher was silent. The teacher's silence didn't mean that the teacher was absent. I was taking a test. I was tempted to raise my hand and ask about a question that was on the test, but I knew the teacher wouldn't give me any answers. Why? Because I was the one taking the test. When we are not being tested, we can ask any question and get an answer, but during the test, there is silence from the teacher.

Spiritual dryness usually is accompanied by this sort of silence from God. When God is silent in your life, that might mean you're taking a test. Remember King Hezekiah: *"God withdrew from him, in order to test him, that He might know all that was in his heart"* (2 Chronicles 32:31). God's silence is not God's absence. It means that we are being tested. One of the things we had to do in school whenever we took a test was to remember what the teacher had taught us before the test. Remembering is the same principle at work in a spiritual wilderness. So often during our dry times, we tend to remember the things we should forget and forget the things we should remember.

God told Israel to celebrate the Passover with a feast to remember how He delivered them from Egypt (Deuteronomy 16:12).

When Israel entered the promised land, God told them to set up a heap of stones for a memorial to remember how they crossed the river Jordan (Joshua 4:3).

David found the courage to face Goliath by remembering how God helped him in the past when he encountered the lion and the bear (1 Samuel 17:37).

# Warfare in the Wilderness

When the disciples were upset about forgetting to take bread into the boat, Jesus reminded them of the miracles of multiplying bread and fish on the land (Mark 8:14, 18-20).

During the Last Supper, our Savior said to His disciples to take communion in remembrance of Him (1 Corinthians 11:24).

It's obvious that God wants us to remember His faithfulness, His Word, and all His glorious works in our life. Faith to get through the spiritual wilderness is found in the victories of the past. Like students, we have to remember what God has said and done to get us through this test. In our minds we must build memorials to His miracles; but instead, some of us build monuments to our mistakes. That's why we are flunking our test in the wilderness. Great faith in dry times is really found in having a good memory of God's past faithfulness and God's promises. David overcame Goliath by remembering God's faithfulness when he encountered the bear and the lion. Jesus overcame the devil in the wilderness by quoting the Scriptures that He remembered.

I'm a huge advocate for remembering and journaling the many spectacular things God has done for us. Past victories contain encouragement for present battles. Another victory-building exercise that's huge in my life is memorizing Scriptures. Whenever I'm in the wilderness or under attack, the Holy Spirit helps me to recall the Scriptures that I memorized which enable me to overcome. Jesus memorized Scriptures; therefore, He was able to quote them to the devil in the wilderness. David said, *"Your word I have hidden in my heart, that I might not sin against You"* (Psalm 119:11). Storing God's Word in our mind through meditation and memorization helps us not to fall in times of a dry season or attack.

# Fight Back

## Demons Don't Dwell in Dry Places

The spiritual world is real. As I mentioned earlier in this book, all physical problems have their roots connected in the spiritual realm. God's enemies, the demons, wage war against people who are His highest creation. We feel the pressure of that warfare by the evil we see in the natural world. When it comes to spiritual warfare, demons and deliverance, Jesus is the best authority on this topic. There is a teaching by Jesus that used to scare me. You have probably heard about demons leaving a person and then returning with seven more wicked demons after a deliverance. Those verses are often used to warn recently delivered people about the dangers of living a life without God. Let's look at these verses closely, and we will learn something about dry places and demons.

*"When an unclean spirit goes out of a man, he goes through dry places, seeking rest, and finds none"* (Matthew 12:43). Did you notice it does not say when the unclean spirit gets cast out of the man? Since demons cannot be everywhere at the same time, they move in and out of a person. That means the person mentioned in this Scripture verse was not totally delivered. He was only relieved from a demon. During a deliverance the demon doesn't leave voluntarily; he is forced out. Demons are cast out during deliverance. The person in this verse experienced only relief, not freedom.

It's much like what happened to King Saul when demons came and left (1 Samuel 16:14-17, 23). They didn't get expelled; they would leave him and come back. Whenever the demons would return, his friends suggested inviting a musician to help him feel better. Instead, they should have invited a prophet or an exorcist to help him bounce back. A spirit that "goes out" is not the same as a spirit getting cast out. I believe when a person is delivered, he or she doesn't fall into the same category this passage is speaking of.

Not only does that evil spirit go out and come back again (which is not consistent with a complete deliverance when evil spirits are cast out), but we also see where the demon goes. According to Scripture, a demon *"goes through dry places, seeking rest, and finds none"* (Matthew 12:43). Demons do not live or abide in dry places; they only go through them. They inhabit people. If you are spiritually dry or you are currently in a spiritual wilderness---do not despair. Maybe you feel tempted by the devil in your wilderness as Jesus was, but don't lose hope. The devil will not stay in a dry place. He will go through it. Demons are seeking a place to rest. So be alert and keep them from finding "rest" in you by praising God, seeking God and standing on His Word, even when you don't feel like it. You may feel tired, but remember, the enemy gets tired too. Your faith, declarations of Scripture verses, and praise wears out the devil. Continue to press into God's presence until the enemy gets restless and moves on. Stand firmly on God's promises and enjoy His warm love in spite of your current situation and feelings.

Something else is worth highlighting---the demon said, *"I will return to my house from which I came"* (Matthew 12:44). This indicates that the person from whom this demon left was formerly the demon's residence. For example, when I travel, I leave my house for a few days or sometimes for a week and I always have a place to come back to because it's my house. I am the owner of it. And that is why I believe the person in Matthew 12 was not saved and delivered, primarily because a saved person is the property of Jesus, bought by the blood of His redemption. Demons do not have the authority to claim ownership or say "my house" when referring to someone who is intimately joined to the Lord as one spirit. *"But he who is joined to the Lord is one spirit with Him"* (1 Corinthians 6:17). A saved person is the temple of the Holy Spirit. Yes, I do believe that demons can torment or oppress a believer, but they cannot possess them as their house.

Furthermore, *"and when he comes, he finds it empty, swept, and put in order"* (Matthew 12:44). This section again confirms that the person referred to in this passage was not saved and delivered. The house is empty, swept and put in order with a behavior modification program. Jesus came to bring us a resurrection that results in an internal transformation. He fills us with His Holy Spirit. He occupies our house. Instead of just sweeping our sins, He removes them. Salvation deals with a man's heart first, not his behavior. Applying self-discipline to put your life in order will work only until the devil comes back. Your own self-discipline has no power to withstand his cunning strategies. Only the Holy Spirit and the powerful blood of Jesus can do that.

The end of the rope for this person is really bad. *"So shall it also be with this wicked generation"* (Matthew 12:45). The demon comes back with seven more demons. It happened to whom? Read verse 45 again. This verse applies to "this wicked generation." The demon returns with seven demons more wicked than himself to a "wicked generation," not to the children of God. Nowhere did Jesus indicate that this ever happens to those who have been saved and delivered. It's for those who have had demons leave them without a total, complete expulsion. It is for the person who did not surrender to Jesus' love but instead modified his or her behavior. Demons make everything worse than before because there is already wickedness at the core of that unsaved person's life. Wicked demons are drawn to wicked people. In Christ, we are a new creation, a royal priesthood and children of God---not wicked.

I believe that after a person gets delivered, demons may return and try to bind him or her again. It's like when Israel had been set free from Pharaoh, but three days later, he pursued them to recapture them and take them back into bondage. Israel was terrified. They thought that their freedom was not going to last. In fact, they doubted that God had finally set them free when they saw Pharaoh reappear with his army on the horizon. Moses told them in their desperate panic to not be afraid, to just keep on marching forward and to watch the salvation of the Lord. While they were watching Pharaoh's army close in behind them, God split the sea before them. Israel marched through on dry land, but Pharaoh with his entire army drowned in the sea. That's the future of every believer who has been set free. God doesn't want you to go back to Egypt but to keep on moving forward to the promised land. Don't let the devil make you doubt your deliverance just because you are being tempted and afflicted by the same issues as before. It doesn't mean that you have not been set free. *"He has delivered us from the power of darkness and transported us into the kingdom of His Son"* (Colossians 1:13). Even if you do fall into the same sin, just repent and get right back up again. You are still righteous in Christ. You are still free. You are still victorious. Just keep moving forward toward your promised land.

The verses in Matthew 12 refer to people who never were delivered or saved, but for those who have only experienced some relief. They never surrendered to Jesus and let Him be the Lord of their life. They may have changed their behavior, but they have not experienced a change in their heart by the work of the Holy Spirit. At the root of it all, they are wicked in their nature and in need of total repentance. They must put their faith completely in Jesus as their Savior.

What I want to encourage you with is that demons roam around in dry places looking for rest. Take courage. When you are in a dry place and feel like you're being tempted by demons, don't give in to the tendency to complain. Instead, confess God's Word. The enemy will not find rest in you and he will leave. *"Then the devil left Him, and behold, angels came and ministered to Him"* (Matthew 4:11). The devil left Jesus and he will also leave you. He doesn't inhabit dry places; he dwells only in wicked places. He lives in dead places. As long as you are alive, even if you're dry, he will feel uncomfortable by your constant praises, praying in the Spirit and confessing God's Word. *"Therefore submit to God. Resist the devil and he will flee from you"* (James 4:7). He will flee if you submit to God's Word and stand your ground. We don't run from the devil; he runs from us. The only thing we run from is sin, not the devil.

If you are in a dry place right now and feel like you're being attacked, I want to prophesy into your life that if you speak God's Word and not your own feelings, the enemy will flee. Remember, you may be dry, but you're not dead.

Finally, your dry season is coming to an end. How do I know this? Because God promises this in the following verses:

> *"I will open rivers in desolate heights, and fountains in the midst of the valleys; I will make the wilderness a pool of water, and the dry land springs of water"* (Isaiah 41:18).

> *"He turns a wilderness into pools of water, and dry land into watersprings"* (Psalm 107:35).

# Warfare in the Wilderness

## Thoughts to Share

*Use #fightbackbook #pastorvlad hashtags.*

If you are losing your hunger for God, force-feed yourself until hunger kicks in.

Remember, repent, and repeat the first works. These are three simple steps to coming back to your "first love."

Many Christians burn out because they neglect to minister to the Lord.

Spiritual hunger follows spiritual feeding.

The period between deliverance and dominion is usually marked by a miserable wilderness.

How we respond in the spiritual wilderness will determine how long we will stay there.

Complaining prolongs your spiritual wilderness; confessing God's Word shrinks it.

When God is silent in your life, that might mean you're taking a test.

So often during our dry times, we tend to remember the things we should forget and forget the things we should remember.

Demons visit dry places, but they settle only in dead places.

*Chapter 6*

# Seek God More Than Freedom

Larry was born and raised in a non-Christian home. The only time he and his family ever attended church was sometimes at Christmas and Easter. Around the age of 9, Larry's mother died leaving him behind with his dad and two sisters. As time passed, Larry's relatives persuaded him to give his life to Jesus and to please them, that's what he did.

Slowly he drifted away from the church, never actually establishing or having a personal relationship with Jesus Christ. As a teenager, Larry started hanging out with some of the guys at school and gradually began to drink and party. As he got older, his drinking problem worsened significantly. At the age of 21, Larry got married and his wife convinced him to start going to church again. One night when they were at church together, they saw the movie called *Left Behind*, where people were dying and going to hell. Larry was frightened; he didn't want to end up like those people who did not know the Lord. That night he accepted Jesus into his life, but once again this did not change Larry.

He went back into living the life he used to live, getting drunk and hanging out at the clubs. He was drunk all the time, every day, never coming home sober. Larry was tired of this kind of lifestyle, hurting his loved ones and not being able to take control of his life. In hopes of becoming a better man, he joined the military. One night in December of 1983, he was leaving the club completely stoned, not even remembering how he got back to the barracks. When he sobered up, his comrades told him that a teenage girl was raped that night. Terrified, Larry didn't know if it was him or not who had done this to the young girl. Even when they confirmed it wasn't him, he was so panic-stricken that he asked his captain to send him to a rehabilitation facility. After his time and treatment there, Larry didn't drink again.

Coming home, he rededicated his life to Jesus. This time he meant business and devoted himself wholeheartedly to the Bible and to Jesus Christ as his Lord. His heart and his entire being started to change. He got to know Jesus more and more, making Him the foundation of his faith. Two years later, Larry was ordained as a deacon in the church he was attending and faithfully served the Lord and his community. Ever since that day in 1983, Larry has never had a single drop of alcohol.

However, Larry still had a smoking problem that he had battled with ever since the age of seventeen, from which he wanted deliverance. Eventually, Larry discovered the Hungry Generation Church, which was still a very young community. During a New Years' service, I was pushing the limits and brought an empty casket into the church. I was giving an illustrated sermon and asked the congregation to write down on a piece of paper what they wanted to get rid of and then throw it into the casket. Larry wrote down "smoking," and God totally delivered him from this problem. It's been fourteen years now since he had his last cigarette. Praise God!

# Fight Back

## In a Battle, She Prepared a Banquet

When Esther came into the presence of the king, he asked her *"What do you wish, Queen Esther? What is your request? It shall be given to you—up to half the kingdom!"* (Esther 5:3). It seemed like this was her moment to tell the king what was really going on because he was waiting to hear her request. Yes, her need was urgent; the lives of all the Jewish people were at stake. Time was of the essence. Anyone else in her situation would have broken down in the presence of the king, asking, begging and pleading for the lives of her nation. Not Esther. She delayed her petition, and instead, invited the king to join her for a special banquet.

*"So Esther answered, 'If it pleases the king, let the king and Haman come today to the banquet that I have prepared for him'"* (Esther 5:4).

It seemed like an odd idea to simply request the king to attend a banquet when really she was in such an intense struggle. It's as though in the presence of this king, she took her eyes off the problem and focused on the king, just to make him happy. She had every reason to blame him for causing the plot since it was he who authorized this horrible plan to slaughter her people. But instead of blaming the king, she decided to feed him.

You as well may be tempted to blame God for not delivering you sooner. You are finding yourself in the same predicament as Esther. God could have prevented that incident from happening to you. A battle is raging right now in your mind, thinking that the all-sovereign God could have prevented that incident. Why didn't He? Maybe you have prayed and fasted for that addiction to be broken, and it seems like your prayers are not being answered. Or maybe you are standing in faith for loved ones and they are only getting worse. Satan, our accuser, will do his best work during these times to discredit God and make Him look bad. He will whisper in your ear as he did to Job's wife, *"Curse God and die"* (Job 2:9). Job thought to himself, if I curse God, then I will die for sure, but if I bless God, I will surely live. He did bless God and lived.

When I was earnestly seeking to be freed from the grip of pornography in my teenage years, I battled with many frustrations concerning God. Questions like, why is God not delivering me already? I prayed. I fasted. I confessed my sin to others. I got an accountability partner. I was tempted to put the blame on God since I was still in bondage. The devil will tempt you to blame God when your deliverance is delayed, *"But each one is tempted when he is drawn away by his own lusts and enticed"* (James 1:14). Don't take his bait to accuse God no matter how much you want to. Instead of blaming God, prepare a feast (of praises) for Him just as Esther did. God is your only hope and God is good. The devil is a liar and his voice is deceiving.

## Don't Use God as a Means to a Goal

Esther didn't use the king to get rid of her enemy right away. She first honored him by providing a feast for him. Her predecessor Vashti didn't honor the king. She didn't come when he commanded her. Instead, Vashti prepared a feast for the women, but Esther prepared a feast for her king.

As believers in the Lord Jesus Christ, we are called to *"love the Lord your God with all your heart, with all your soul, and with all your mind"* (Matthew 22:37-38). *"This is the first and great commandment."* When bad habits, addictions, or spiritual chains seem to keep us in a chokehold, we forget about His commandment. It's good to desire freedom, but we must want God more! Otherwise, we will only be using God as a means to reach freedom. God doesn't want to be a means to a goal, even if that goal is deliverance. God wants to be your goal! The first and great commandment is not to use the Lord your God to get free but to love the Lord your God.

When Esther requested the king's presence at a banquet instead of discussing for what was really bothering her, she was communicating to the king that he was much more important than the crisis she was facing. The king was more powerful than the predicament that she was in. Her husband, the king, was the only one able to do something about her dilemma. She knew that panic and desperation would not be the most effective way to go about getting deliverance. We should learn the same from her strategy. Focus more on God than on your bondage. In spite of your current spiritual trouble, remember that God is your goal, not just a means to the goal for a better life. *"But seek first the kingdom of God and His righteousness, and all these things will be added to you"* (Matthew 6:33). God promised us freedom and abundant life; but much more, He is our God whom we love, not somebody to use.

If your whole mind is wrapped up in your bondage, then God is no longer your primary focus. People get totally desperate for God when they are in bondage, but so often, the moment the burden is removed, their desperation disappears as well! It's because they are not desperate for God but only desperate for freedom. They use God as a means to find freedom and then leave Him once they have met their goal, which wasn't having a deep relationship with God but getting free from their problem.

# Seek God More Than Freedom

## Israel Used God;
## Moses Used Deliverance

That was my experience in my teen years. I was addicted to pornography. My bondage to guilt and repeated cycles of sin produced desperation in my heart to get free. I was so sick and tired of those chains. I wanted it all to end, so I humbled myself and drew near to God through prayer and fasting. I prayed daily and fasted every Wednesday because I really wanted to be free. God was gracious to me and freed me from that bondage by showing me what real love is. However, as time passed I noticed my fervency, my drive, and appetite for the things of God diminished and that perplexed me. While I was struggling, my heart burned for God but once I was free and doing better, I became complacent and indifferent.

After much soul searching and praying, the Holy Spirit showed me what my motive really was. Although I was so tired and embarrassed with my sin and wanted to have peace in my heart with a clear conscience, I was only pursuing freedom - not God. I was praying and fasting for freedom. I didn't really want God as much as I wanted deliverance. That's why, after I got what I wanted from God, He was no longer "needed." That was a hard lesson for me. I used Him only as a means to my goal, but He was not my primary goal. When I realized that He was not my primary goal, I repented and asked the Holy Spirit to change my motives and heart's desire. The cry of my heart became, "God, I want You more than I want freedom. You are not just my means to a goal. You are my ultimate goal, my reward, my all!" Today, I am not at all perfect when it comes to the pursuit of God, but with the help of the Holy Spirit, my love for the Lord is greater now than when I was in bondage.

# Fight Back

This reminds me of the Israelites when they experienced the exodus from Egypt. Not long after their deliverance, they built a golden calf and worshipped it. Reading the accounts in Exodus, Numbers, Leviticus, and Deuteronomy, I don't see much spiritual desire toward God on their part. They cried out to God while in bondage, but it wasn't God that they really wanted. They wanted relief from their pain and suffering, and who would blame them for desiring to have a better life? God showed them His majestic glory in order to draw them close to Himself so that they would fall in love with Him. But throughout the entire forty years in the wilderness, they complained, whined and rebelled against God. The desperation for God that they felt in Egypt wasn't there in the wilderness. To them, God was only a means to get out of bondage. God was not their primary goal.

Moses was different though. After seeing all the miracles and signs which God performed in Egypt through him, he hungered for God even more. *"And he said, 'Please, show me Your glory'"* (Exodus 33:18). All the amazing power that Moses had witnessed whetted his appetite for God. You can see that Israel only used God to get out of Egypt because after deliverance, they had little desire for God Himself. However, Moses used the exodus from Egypt and all the miracles God did to pursue Him more. He was already close to God and his request was to *"Show me Your glory."* He wasn't asking for an easy road to the promised land. Moses didn't view God as a means to get a better life. When God said that he wouldn't accompany Israel on their journey because of their rebellion, but would instead send an angel, Moses responded, *"If Your Presence does not go with us, do not bring us up from here"* (Exodus 33:15). Through this, I see that Moses cared more about the abiding Presence of God and less about the promised land.

# Seek God More Than Freedom

Deliverance is important. Freedom is vital. It's what God promised you. But there is a danger of actually not wanting God Himself but only the blessings that He gives. That's why you shouldn't focus on your freedom as much as you focus on the Lord. He will deliver you, and if God is not your aim, your passion for Him will dwindle. Be like Esther; when she needed freedom, she focused on giving the king a banquet.

## A Banquet is Better Than Begging

Here is something I shared in my *Single, Ready to Mingle* book. I remember one time when I hit a pretty dry season in prayer, and I felt that routinely coming to God was a burden to me. I would wake up early in the morning to pray, but I wanted to quit because I saw no point in making all that effort. I told God that it would be better for both of us if I just stopped coming to Him in prayer since it wasn't doing me any good. Then I felt in my heart God reply to me, "I love your presence more than you could ever love Mine." I knew that I loved God's presence, but God loving my presence was something new for me. Wow! Then I realized that God treasured my company and He loved having me being there with Him. He paid a price to have me. It costs me nothing to have God, but it cost Him everything to have me. Whenever I don't feel God's presence for some time, I come and sit and wait patiently for Him. I remind Him that since He loves me so much, I just want to be with Him. In fact, one time I prayed this prayer, "Lord I don't feel you. I have not felt you in a while, but I am here. I know you love me. I know that you treasure my company. So, here I am. Enjoy me. I am all yours." Then right after that, God's glory flooded my soul. God loves my presence! He treasures my company!

# Fight Back

And that's what Esther did; she prepared a banquet for the king. She didn't wait for him to take her on a date. So many times we think that spending time with God is about us enjoying God's presence. We use prayer to get back into contact with Him and that's good. But we need to remind ourselves that it's all about Him. *"For the Lord takes pleasure in His people"* (Psalm 149:4). The Lord delights in you, he takes pleasure in you. Therefore, it's time to prepare a feast for Him. Bring yourself to God, your heart, mind, and body. He enjoys your companionship. He delights in you. Instead of feeling discouraged whenever you don't sense His presence, let God enjoy your presence. Prepare Him a feast. It's about Him, not you. As you take your eyes off yourself, you will be surprised how He will shower you with his delightful glory and grace.

The king was delighted to come to the feast. In fact, he kept on asking Esther, "What can I do for you?" I believe that when we make God our primary goal in life, letting Him enjoy our company, He will pour out His favor. Freedom will flow like a river in our lives. We live for His glory, for His pleasure. *"You are worthy, O Lord our God, to receive glory and honor and power. For you created all things, and they exist because you created what you pleased."* (Revelation 4:11, *New Living Translation*).

When you feel under attack, discouraged and defeated, make a banquet for the Lord. Maybe everything in you might be screaming that God is the one who should prepare a table for you, not you for Him. Remember, whether in good times or bad, we exist for His glory and His pleasure. When you prepare Him a banquet and the king asks, "What can I do for you?" let Him enjoy you rather than you begging Him for something.

Solomon had a similar experience. *"Solomon went up to the bronze altar in the Lord's presence...and sacrificed*

# Seek God More Than Freedom

*1,000 burnt offerings on it. That night God appeared to Solomon and said to him, 'Ask! What shall I give you?'"* (2 Chronicles 1:6-7). Solomon was young and inexperienced. He was in desperate need of God's help. This young king was filling the shoes of Israel's beloved King David. Oh, how he needed God's grace! Solomon did it right. Instead of panic, desperation, or begging God, he simply honored Him with a huge banquet. God came in a dream that night and inquired, "What do you want? Ask, and I will give it to you." We all want God to ask us what we want, but the key is - prepare a banquet instead of begging.

Worship the Lord instead of whining.

Confess God's faithfulness instead of complaining.

Focus on the Lord when you're tempted to focus only on yourself.

Jesus assured us that if we seek the Kingdom of God first and his righteousness that He will add the rest of the things (Matthew 6:33). Don't seek a breakthrough, freedom, or a miracle more than seeking God Himself. *"Delight yourself also in the Lord, and He shall give you the desires of your heart"* (Psalm 37:4). Prepare a banquet for the Lord when you feel in bondage.

These banquets are prepared with thanksgiving, worship and praise. Thanksgiving and praise are the protocol for entering God's presence.

*"Enter His gates with thanksgiving; and into His courts with praise. Give thanks to Him and praise His name"* (Psalm 100:4).

# Fight Back

## Seek God, Not Open Doors

In Christian circles where deliverance is practiced, there is a great emphasis on open doors to the demonic enemy. In fact, sometimes it's taken to extremes. People shift their focus from the Lord to focusing on finding an open door. I firmly believe our actions and behavior can open a door the devil and that repentance will close that door. However, living in a constant search for an open door in your life is not scriptural. We are called to seek the Lord's face. He will reveal what must be repented of, or renounced and when He leads us to repent and renounce our sin, He enables us to close that doors to the enemy permanently.

When I was addicted to porn, I fasted for seven days. The Lord showed me that my first exposure to porn was an open door, and the second time I was exposed a few years later was also an open door. I saw a vision of my soulish house having a front door and a back door, the front door being my first exposure and the back door being the second exposure. Right then and there, I repented and renounced my addiction. I truly believed that those doors were closed and locked. The fruit of my repentance testifies to that. What I want to highlight is that I was not looking for an open door; I just knew that there was something wrong with me. While seeking the Lord's face, the Holy Spirit showed me what needed to be dealt with and how.

Constant digging into the past, when the Holy Spirit does not lead us to do so, makes us spiritual archaeologists, not sons and daughters. In fact, we are warned against looking into our past. *"No one, having put his hand to the plow, and looking back, is fit for the kingdom of God"* (Luke 9:62).

## Seek God More Than Freedom

*"Remember Lot's wife"* (Luke 17:32). She tried to walk forward by looking backward and suddenly became a pillar of salt. We are called to be people of salt not pillars of salt. When we always look back, we become monuments instead of movements.

*"But one thing I do, forgetting those things which are behind and reaching forward to those things which are ahead"* (Philippians 3:13) was Paul's secret. He did not dig into the past but pressed on into the Lord's calling for his life.

It's clear that we are to glance at our past but keep our gaze constantly upon the Lord. There's a reason that the windshield in our car is bigger than the rearview mirror. We can safely drive only by looking forward. Where we're going to is so much better than where we've come from. The main reason we should ever glance into our past is to glorify God for what He has already done and to learn whatever lessons He wants to teach us. Remember His faithfulness in your past so that you can build up faith for the present battle. Maybe the Holy Spirit will reveal something that needs to be uprooted, repented of, or forgiven. But the constant obsession with the past is dangerous, and it never leads to freedom. It's like a revolving door. You feel there's no end to repenting. People obsessed with the past go from deliverance to deliverance, and rarely go on to dominion. Your victory is not in your past but in your future.

Seek the Lord, not the door.

# Fight Back

## "I Shot the President, But Doctors Killed Him"

I heard a story of the twentieth President of the United States, James Garfield, who was shot four months after becoming a president. As President Garfield was getting ready to board a train, he was shot by a crazy guy. In those days presidents didn't have security personnel[8]. While bleeding on the train station floor, several doctors arrived on the scene to examine him and tried to locate the bullet in his body. The injury that the president received was a survivable injury, but well-meaning physicians only worsened the damage by using their unsterilized fingers and instruments to probe the wound, which introduced germs and caused infections.

Not being able to find the bullet, they took him to the White House where they continued to treat him. Doctor Williard Bliss administered medicine and tried other means to locate the bullet. The doctor even got help from the famous inventor, Alexander Graham Bell, who used his metal detector trying to locate the bullet. This machine failed to work because the president was lying on a bed made of metal springs which caused interference during the screening. All those attempts were futile. To make things worse, Dr. Bliss only permitted a search on the right side of the president's body, where he incorrectly believed the bullet was lodged.

Not long after that, President Garfield died. The one who shot him was found guilty of murder and sentenced to death by hanging. There is some truth to what the assassin claimed, "The doctors killed Garfield, I just shot him."

---

[8] Written by Evan Andrew, Nov.30, 2018 (Accessed on May 13, 2020). www.history.com/news/the-assassination-of-president-james-a-garfield

# Seek God More Than Freedom

He probably could have survived with a bullet lodged in his body if they would have stopped digging for it. I see similar issues with believers who are obsessively digging into their past looking for hidden secrets that might enable them to live happily in the present. All that does is leads us to spiritual infection. Once you open your book of life to look for sin, you don't have to look far; you will find what you're looking for. You will repent over the same thing again and again and again. Then the enemy will question the authenticity of your faith and repentance. All of this undermines the power of the blood of Jesus over your past sins. Your obsessive focus on your sinful self takes your mind away from seeking Christ and gives the enemy power. From my experience, I have yet to meet someone who walks in victory who is always looking in the rearview mirror. Spiritual archaeologists go from deliverance to deliverance, not from deliverance to dominion.

## Focus on Being Filled More Than Being Free

Growing people change. Growing in the Lord brings not only freedom but ongoing victory. My brother who was addicted to drugs for seven years had a powerful encounter with the Lord one night. He surrendered his life to Jesus, gave up drugs and his rebellious life and asked my parents for forgiveness. But he still struggled to overcome a few things from the past. In my life group, I would encourage him to not focus on freedom but to focus on being filled with God's Word and His holy presence. I knew that he tried his best to quit the bad habits he had picked up in the past, but trying harder was not the solution. He would have to try something totally different in order to get different results. One of the reasons he kept on failing was because he was spiritually empty on the inside. When he started to fill himself with God's Word and dedicate himself to prayer, then freedom and victory came as a result.

So, focus on being filled with an awareness of God more than on just being free. There are lessons from God that will come as you grow in Him. I share more about that in my *Break Free* book in the chapter titled "As You Grow." The stories and scriptures in it refer to God's promises to fully deliver you as you grow in Him. *"Being confident of this thing, that He who has begun a work in you will complete it until the day of Jesus Christ"* (Philippians 1:6).

My late uncle Stephen, who co-founded the church with my pastor, had an accident in his youth. When he was a young man and not serving God, he was making a bomb to blow fish out of the lake. Something went wrong, and the bomb exploded in his house, blowing off the roof and rendering him blind in one eye and cutting some of his fingers. Glass from the explosive penetrated his body. Decades later, little shards of glass would emerge from his skin. He wasn't looking for them; they simply came to the surface as he grew older. Scripture says, *"There is no fear in love, but perfect love casts out fear"* (1 John 4:18). The word "perfect" can be translated as grown-up or mature love. There are some things that can be cast out by maturing in God's love. As you grow in the awareness of the Lord, certain things leave you. Whatever fragments of glass that remain in you from your past will come out as you mature in God's love and His Word.

If you repented, renounced sin, and the Holy Spirit is not bringing it to your attention, don't become obsessed over it. Focus on growing in the Lord. *"But to you who fear My name, the Sun of Righteousness shall arise, with*

# Seek God More Than Freedom

*healing in His wings; and you shall go out and grow fat like stall-fed calves. You shall trample the wicked, for they shall be ashes under the soles of your feet"* (Malachi 4:2-3). Have you noticed that if we fear the Lord, we will go out and grow as fat calves? Now, I know fat is not something we desire physically, but to be well-fed spiritually is good. In fact, it's so good that those fat calves who represent us will trample on the wicked, and the wicked will be like ashes under our feet.

My friend, it's time to get "fat" on God's Word so that we can walk in daily victory.

## In the Presence of My Enemies

*"If it pleases the king, let the king and Haman come today to the banquet that I have prepared for him"* (Esther 5:4). Imagine that! Esther invited her enemy Haman to the banquet she prepared for the king. *"Then the king said, 'Bring Haman quickly, that he may do as Esther has said.' So the king and Haman went to the banquet that Esther had prepared"* (Esther 5:5). Haman actually showed up to Esther's banquets two days in a row! God put it into Esther's heart to delay her petition for one more day; she did not know, but God did, what was going to happen that very night (Esther 6:1-14).

Esther experienced what David wrote about in Psalm 23:5, *"You prepare a table before me in the presence of my enemies."* She had to learn to eat in the presence of her enemy. Like the song, written by Bethel Worship (Jonathan David Helser, Melissa Helser, Molly Skaggs, and Raquel Vega) says,

I raise a hallelujah, in the presence of my enemies.

I raise a hallelujah, louder than the unbelief.

# Fight Back

I raise a hallelujah, my weapon is a melody.

I raise a hallelujah, Heaven comes to fight for me.

I believe all of us, like Esther, in some season of our life will have to learn to raise a "hallelujah" in the presence of our enemies. Don't wait until the enemy is gone before you start to eat in the presence of your king. Don't wait until you get out of prison to start praying and singing praises to God. Maybe you feel unworthy to sit and eat at God's table. Perhaps guilt and shame are staring you in the face while you're seated at God's table of grace. Don't starve yourself because the enemy is present.

Earlier in this chapter, I mentioned that we must make a banquet of worship to God when we are in a battle. Now, I want to shift your focus to eating from the Lord's table in the presence of your enemies. If the "Haman" of insecurity, fear, and anxiety come to your banquet, go ahead and enjoy what the Lord has prepared for you in His presence. Don't let anything like guilt and shame keep you away from feeding on God's Word. Don't abandon the banquet of God's table even if you know the enemy is present.

I remember being at a large conference and two of the invited speakers had an ongoing personal feud. Only later did I find out about this conflict. When we got to the Green Room, one speaker was there, but the other one had left. I thought that he must be tired and had gone to his room to rest. But later I found out that the moment he saw his enemy-friend at the conference, he must have thought, "I can't stay here if he is here." So, he vanished. It's embarrassing that this exists in Christian circles.

It's even worse when we don't go to God's table because the accuser is present. We don't feel up to reading our Bible because the sins that we have committed make us feel ashamed or indifferent. We make promises to ourselves that we will clean up our life first, and then we will be worthy to be seated at His table. But it's impossible to clean a dirty window with a dirty rag. We can't clean ourselves up. The only thing that can wash us clean is the blood of Jesus and the cleansing power of God's Word. Jesus lovingly invites us to come to His table the way we are. But we will go away hungry if we believe the lie that our failures and sin disqualify us from being seated there.

There is a seat at God's table for you. Don't let Haman intimidate you by his presence that makes you feel unworthy to be there. Nobody has to apply soap after he washes or has to go to the hospital after he gets healthy.

## Covered by the Table

There is a beautiful story of Mephibosheth who was the son of Jonathan, King David's best friend. As a child, Mephibosheth became crippled when his nurse dropped him while running. David had made a covenant with Mephibosheth's dad. *"So David said to him, 'Do not fear, for I will surely show you kindness for Jonathan your father's sake, and will restore to you all the land of Saul your grandfather; and you shall eat bread at my table continually'"* (2 Samuel 9:7).

He was invited to be at the table only because of the covenant between David and Jonathan. It wasn't because he was worthy, and that's the same with us. We are seated in heavenly places in Christ, not because of our worthiness but because of Jesus' covenant with the Father (Ephesians 2:6). Therefore, the enemy has no right to keep us from being seated at the Lord's table because of our faults or failures. Unfortunately, so often we excuse

# Fight Back

ourselves from being seated due to our sense of "un-worthiness." Some of us just don't want to eat in the presence of our enemies.

*"So Mephibosheth dwelt in Jerusalem, for he ate continually at the king's table. And he was lame in both his feet"* (2 Samuel 9:13). Mephibosheth didn't let his disabled feet keep him away from sitting at the king's table. In fact, even though sitting there didn't cure his problem, he continued returning to the table. He wasn't cured by sitting there, but his lame feet were covered by that table. When you continually sit at the table of the Lord, whatever makes you feel unworthy will be covered by His grace and favor. Don't avoid the banquet just because Haman is present.

Enjoy the banquet!

# Seek God More Than Freedom

## Thoughts to Share
*Use #fightbackbook #pastorvlad hashtags.*

God doesn't want to be a means to a goal, even if that goal is deliverance.

Worship the Lord instead of whining.

Constant digging in the past without the Holy Spirit's guidance makes us spiritual archaeologists, not sons and daughters.

Growing in the Lord brings not only freedom but also an ongoing victory.

Don't wait until the enemy is gone before you start to eat in the presence of your king.

*Chapter 7*

# **Remove the Mask**

At the age of four, something tragic happened to Geovanna. She became a victim of molestation. The result of this situation brought devastating consequences to her life. She fell into a cycle of depression and anxiety which negatively affected her relationships, sleep and self-esteem.

At the age of twelve, Geovanna began to notice other girls and felt attracted to them, but it wasn't until high school that she started to pursue relationships with girls. She also started to party, get drunk and use weed. There were many hopeless nights where she considered ending her own life. One night, completely broken, she purchased a bottle of pills hoping to end it all. With the bottle still in hand, she suddenly stopped herself. Something deep down inside called her to hold on because there was more to her life than she could ever imagine.

Not too long after this moment, she was invited through Facebook to our "Raised to Deliver" conference with Hungry Generation. At the meeting, she began to manifest, but that wasn't the end of her deliverance because in her heart she had not fully surrendered to the Lord. The Lord didn't give up on her and faithfully pursued Geovanna.

The Monday after the conference, we had a meeting where we prayed for our volunteers and Geovanna attended that meeting. She was both mentally and emotionally exhausted from living that lifestyle. Geovanna was tired of feeling like she couldn't win against depression, anxiety, and same-sex attraction that ate away at her daily. By this time, she was fully ready to give all of herself to the Lord. She had enough! With all her heart, Geovanna finally decided to let go and give it all to God.

The Lord radically delivered her and she came to know freedom. That freedom was so pure and filled with joy. Completely free from same-sex attraction, the peace she felt after her deliverance outweighed every bit of darkness. God continues to teach her how to fight back when depression tries to sneak in again.

Through prayer, time with the Lord and learning to hear His voice, she continues to enjoy total freedom. Now, Geovanna walks in victory and boldness. She loves sharing her testimony with others who are in the same bondage she suffered before her freedom. She wants to show people how to live a fulfilling life with Jesus, free from anxiety.

## Confession is Good for the Soul

Confession is good for the soul, says the old cliche. It has some truth in it. St Augustine said, "Confession of evil works is the beginning of good works." Even though as protestants we don't practice confessionals, the principle of confessing our sins has great sanctifying power.

When Esther was taken to the palace for a beauty pageant, *"Esther had not revealed her people or family, for Mordecai had charged her not to reveal it"* (Esther 2:10). She was an orphan and Mordecai, who worked at the king's palace, was her cousin. Heeding the instructions of her cousin, she kept her Jewish ancestry a secret. And it was a secret until the occasion when she hosted the second banquet for the king.

# Fight Back

As the king was insistent on granting her wish and request, she revealed her past and the secret that she had kept all this time. We don't see the king punishing Esther for revealing the secret. In fact, all the anger was directed at Haman for his evil plot, not at Esther for her confession. *"Then the king arose in his wrath from the banquet of wine and went into the palace garden; but Haman stood before Queen Esther, pleading for his life, for he saw that evil was determined against him by the king"* (Esther 7:7).

So many people, when dealing with internal bondage, are afraid to be honest with God, fearing his displeasure with their confession. But nothing is hidden from God's eyes. Really, he wants to see his children trust him. They must believe that he will show them grace when they confess their sins. Just be honest and transparent with God. *"If we confess our sins, He is faithful and just to forgive us our sins and to cleanse us from all unrighteousness"* (1 John 1:9).

## Secret Sins Make Us Sick

In my e-book *From Secret Sin to Secret Place*, I mentioned how some believers live as soldiers of Christ publicly, but privately they live as slaves to their own passions of lust, pride and other secret sins.

Sin has this ugly tendency to hide. This is how it works: When a person sins, he feels guilty for what he did. Guilt leads to shame. Shame leads to secrecy. And because the sin is hidden, the person is now being deceived to commit that sin again. "Nobody's going to see it anyway" is the usual lie. It is a lie because *"For nothing is secret that will not be revealed, nor anything hidden that will not be known and come to light"* (Luke 8.17). Sooner or later what we do in secret will become public. But that should not be our motivation to confess our sins. We confess our bondage to secret sin because the Holy Spirit gives us a conviction to do so, not because of fear of getting caught.

If we hold on to our secret sin, it makes us sick on the inside. King David experienced this very well. He wrote, *"When I kept silent, my bones grew old through my groaning all the day long. For day and night Your hand was heavy upon me; my vitality was turned into the drought of summer"* (Psalm 32:3-4). Secret sin and silence lead to sickness in the soul and body. We become emotionally ill and possibly mentally ill. Even our physical body takes a toll from the sin that we hide. Unconfessed sin saps our energy.

At one summer camp where I preached, I showed the youth an illustration of what hiding secret sin does to us. I had a young fellow put on a backpack and then I filled that backpack with heavy rocks. The young man almost fell backward due to the weight of the rocks. Next, I closed the backpack. I reminded the young people sitting in front of him that they could not see the rocks because they were hidden inside the backpack. In fact, some of the ones in front of him couldn't even see the backpack. But what everyone did see was how uncomfortable that person was with the heavy load. He was tense and getting tired. It took a lot of energy for him just to stand due to the weight of those rocks. Then I asked him to run. He looked at me in shock. He tried to run, but it was hard on his physical body. I explained that's what secret sin does to our soul. It drains us of spiritual strength. It slows us down in our pursuit of God. People don't run toward God because it's hard to run with a weight on their back. I continued to point out that it's not the race that is hard, but that it's our heart that is heavy.

That's why the author of Hebrews says, *"let us lay aside every weight and the sin which so easily ensnares us, and let us run with endurance the race that is set before us"* (Hebrew 12:1). It's you who has to lay aside every weight so that you can run the race. If you think Christianity is hard, maybe it's because your heart is heavy. Perhaps you're carrying the weight of unconfessed sin and that your inner struggle weighs you down. Secret sin makes us spiritually sick and slow.

David testifies, *"I acknowledged my sin to You, and my iniquity I have not hidden. I said, 'I will confess my transgressions to the Lord,' and You forgave the iniquity of my sin"* (Psalm 32:5). He acknowledged, he refused to hide, he confessed. And look at God's response: *"You forgave me."* That's what God is going to do for you as well.

## Remove the Mask, Not the Crown

When we were born again, our spirit was made alive: *"Even when we were dead in trespasses, He made us alive together with Christ"* (Ephesians 2:5). He made us perfect forever by the one and only sacrifice of Jesus (Hebrews 10:14). In fact, our spirit is joined with Jesus Himself and that's why it's perfect: *"He who is joined to the Lord is one spirit with Him"* (1 Corinthians 6:17). God has given us the Holy Spirit as a seal or signature ring mark, to be His irreversible pledge that we belong to Him (Ephesians 1:13). Since we are a spirit-being (our real self), God sees us as perfect even as Jesus Himself is perfect since our spirit is joined with Him and becomes one with the Lord Jesus. *"He has reconciled you by Christ's physical body through death to present you holy, and blameless, and irreproachable in His sight"* (Colossians 1:22). That's such powerful news. All of that is possible because of Jesus' death on the cross.

Even though our human spirit is perfect, our soul and body are not. Our soul is always being perfected. It's still being saved by the renewing of our minds. *"For by one offering He has perfected forever those who are being sanctified"* (Hebrews 10:14). We are perfect forever. Let that sink in, not perfect until you make your next mistake. Not perfect until you sin again. It's forever! God's love for you doesn't change when you fall. Although our spirit is perfect forever, we are continuously being sanctified in our souls. We are already perfect in our spirit but being perfected in our soul (the seat of our mind, will and emotions).

Many Christians are unsure of their salvation in Jesus. They feel that every time they sin, they lose their salvation. So they need to confess their sin quickly to get their salvation back. I lived with my parents for twenty-four years until I got married. In twenty-four years of my life, I made mistakes, I provoked them to anger, I said things I regret now and I did things I wish I had never done.

Do you know that not once did they disown me? Also, do you know that not once did I think that they would get rid of me? Their love for me was unconditional. I didn't deserve it or earn it. In fact, they loved me with this perfect love when I was born to them as a child. Even though I was an infant, totally helpless, I was loved even before I was able to talk, walk, and be useful in the house. My parents are not perfect, but my place in their hearts as a son is secure forever. That will never change. Unless of course, I could choose to disown them and renounce my last name and totally leave them.

# Fight Back

## Gym vs Family

Salvation is called new birth. It's a birth into God's kingdom. We are born into God's family, and therefore God is our heavenly Father. You cannot join God's family; you must be born into it. You can join a local church, but God's kingdom has only one entrance which is "birth." Jesus called it the new birth. This occurs by trusting in Jesus' death on the cross for our sins as the only means of our salvation.

Being part of a family is different from being a member of a club.

When I joined a local gym, I agreed with the rules and payments and based on this, I became a member of that gym. Each month I pay my monthly fees and I enjoy access to that facility. But if I don't pay my monthly dues, my access card will stop functioning. I will no longer have access to the gym.

Also, if I break one of the rules, my membership will be terminated. That is how membership in a club works.

Membership in my father's family is different. I didn't need to qualify to become his son. I didn't have to agree to any rules that let me earn a place in the Savchuk household. There were no prior requirements for me to be accepted, welcomed and cared for. I didn't have to keep rules to gain their love. Neither did I have to make monthly payments to maintain my place in the household.

Don't get me wrong. When I grew up, my parents set boundaries in the house. I had chores to do and a curfew to keep. We had rules, but they were not established to gain my sonship nor did breaking them cost me my position as a son in the family.

# Remove the Mask

In the gym, rules condition my relationship with the gym. In my family, rules confirm my relationship with my family.

In the gym, rules are to join the gym. In the family, rules come after birth.

In the gym, breaking the rules meant losing membership. In the family, breaking the rules meant time out.

In the gym, I pay monthly fees to keep my membership. In the family, it's about keeping a relationship.

When I broke rules in the family, I didn't lose my family. I lost certain privileges. We had certain disciplines such as spankings when I was younger. When I grew older, my parents would limit particular privileges that I could enjoy. When we as believers break God's commandments, there are certain consequences, but losing our salvation and God as our father is not one of them.

God does not punish us for our sins - that already happened on the cross. God punished Jesus for all of our sins - past, present, and future. But if and when we break His house rules, our loving Father disciplines us to develop within us the fruit of holiness.

Punishment is different than discipline:

Punishment is eternal, discipline is temporary.

Punishment is for sinners, discipline is for saints.

Punishment is out of wrath, discipline is out of love.

Punishment is later, discipline is now.

Punishment casts a person out of God's presence, discipline draws him or her closer.

People in this world who don't live according to God's commandments will go to eternal separation from Him, even if it seems like their sins do not get them in trouble while here on earth. But when we as Christians refuse to walk in obedience as God's children, our Father will discipline us, here and now, to develop within us an obedient character that lines up with God's character.

Again, keeping the rules doesn't make our relationship with God conditional. It's a positive confirmation of that relationship. Breaking His guidelines does not disqualify us from God's family. Breaking His rules doesn't put us out of the house. We might experience a spiritual "time out" or His discipline but all of that is out of His fatherly love. God draws us closer to Himself to produce in us His character.

## The Righteous Falls Seven Times

Getting saved does not mean we will never sin again. The righteous man falls seven times and gets back up (Proverbs 24:16). In other words, we do not stop being righteous because we fall. Jesus is the one who makes us righteous; it's not our efforts to "never fall again." Righteousness is not a guarantee that falling will never happen; it's an assurance that we will get back up again when we do fall.

Righteousness is our right-standing with God (a gift) which leads to right- living before God. Right-living is a process that takes time. Right-standing is our status but right-living is our daily state of being.

For example, when I was born, I immediately became a son to my parents. Sonship wasn't earned or worked for. It came with birth. It was a gift. That's why when the prodigal son tried to say to his father in repentance, *"Father, I have sinned against heaven and in your sight, and am no longer worthy to be called your son"* (Luke 15:21), his father didn't let him finish with that conclusion; he told the servants to prepare a feast. The prodigal son's repentance was real and genuine, but he was wrong about one thing. You are not a son by worth; you're a son by birth. I became a son by birth, not by worth. The position which I occupy in the heart of my parents will never change. I am their son.

When I learned how to speak and walk, I was still their son.

When I went to school and graduated, I was still their son.

When I got my license and got my first job, I was still their son.

When I got married and moved out of their house, I continued being their son.

My status as a son didn't improve or get upgraded as I grew up. The position of sonship in my parents' home provided me with love, care, and a place where I could grow from a baby to a student, to an employee, to a husband, and now to a pastor. All the growth that I am still experiencing doesn't make me more of a "son." I am still the same son today as I was when I was a baby. Growing up didn't make me more of a son to my parents; being born did.

That's how righteousness works. It's stable, secure and doesn't change even though our habits, character and attitude do change. Living righteously develops over time. You change gradually. Spiritual growth is only possible when you are securely anchored in the righteousness that is given to you at your second birth.

# Fight Back

Growth comes naturally, both physically and spiritually. We grow slowly but surely. Just as a baby eats, cries and sleeps, we grow by eating from God's Word, by crying out to God in prayer and sleeping in the assurance of God's grace. As I grew, I learned to walk, speak and develop good habits from the training and love of my caring parents. I didn't want to stay a toddler all my life. I didn't want to suck my mother's breast at thirteen or be pushed in a stroller at the age of twenty-five. Growth is natural for those who are alive and well. So, growing in right-living is natural to those who are righteous.

That's why Proverbs tell us that a righteous man falls but gets up. His new spirit doesn't want to sin, but his soul is still being sanctified. The gift of righteousness doesn't make it impossible to sin, but it makes it impossible to stay in that sin. Those who are made new in Christ look for ways to overcome sin, not an excuse to live in it. *"No one who is born of God will continue to sin, because God's seed [nature] remains in him; he cannot go on sinning because he has been born of God. This is how we know who the children of God are"* (1 John 3:9-10 NIV). Your failure is not your identity. Sin is not your identity. Jesus is your identity.

When a sheep falls into the mud, it begins to cry out, but when a pig falls into the mud, it plays in it. We are sheep, not pigs. Satan uses sin to bring over us guilt and shame. He causes us to doubt our salvation and question God's love for us. He wants us to hide from God as Adam did and blame others for our sin so that we don't receive the grace we need for overcoming it.

Dear reader, you are not looking for an excuse to remain in bondage. If you were, you wouldn't be reading this book. Don't let the devil lie to you saying that God's grace has been exhausted by your weakness and many failures. My own brother who was on drugs for seven years lived in my parent's house. He brought so much pain to them because of his actions and attitude. They didn't disown him; they didn't kick him out of their house. They loved him, spoke to him and prayed and cared for him. They also suffered because of him. After seven years, he came back to himself and repented. They forgave him. It's the love and mercy that they showed to their son that helped him to overcome the bondage that he was in.

For those of you who are accusing me in your heart that I am giving people a license to sin, let me remind you that sinners don't need a license to sin. They sin without the license. No, God's grace does not give a license to sin; it gives the power to overcome sin. Guilt, shame, fear, and doubt don't give you power over sin. They only empower sin. God uses grace, not guilt, to help us out of our sin. That's why Jesus told the woman caught in the act of adultery, *"Neither do I condemn you; go and sin no more"* (John 8:11). Do you see how His first statement is *"I don't condemn you,"* followed by *"go and sin no more"*? That is the secret. If you want to go and sin no more, you must embrace Jesus' gift of "no condemnation." If you leave His presence feeling condemned, you will sin again! Condemnation leads to more sin. Grace empowers you to overcome sin.

If you fall into the same sin again and again, get up. People don't drown by falling into the water; they drown by staying there. So, get up! Confess it to God; confess it to someone you trust; receive His mercy, and forgive yourself. Don't wallow in guilt and shame as though your self-inflicted punishment will make you feel better. If Jesus' sacrifice wasn't enough for your sin, He would have told you. If His death on the cross were not sufficient, He would ask you to add your personal suffering to His atonement. His death was enough. His sacrifice was sufficient. You don't need to hurt yourself to prove to God that you are truly sorry. Unlike others, God can read your mind and read your heart. He knows your heart. Stop punishing yourself. His punishment on the cross was enough.

## The Cross Took Care of
## the Past, Present, and Future

What gives me the courage to get up when I fall is knowing that Jesus' sacrifice was sufficient. His death on the cross didn't just pay for the sins of the past but for the present and future ones as well.

*"And every priest stands ministering daily and offering repeatedly the same sacrifices, which can never take away sins. But this Man, after He had offered one sacrifice for sins forever, sat down at the right hand of God"* (Hebrews 10:11-12). Unlike the Old Testament priests who had to offer sacrifices every year for their own sins first and then for the sins of people, Jesus by one offering took care of all our sins - forever. Think about it, when Jesus was dying on the cross for our sins two thousand years ago, all our sins were at that time future sins. What you see as your past sins were "your future sins" when Jesus died two thousand years ago. Every time you sin, Jesus doesn't come again and again to die for every sin. He did it only once for all the sins of the past, present, and future. That's why He is greater than any priest of the Old Testament. He is not only our priest but also the perfect sacrifice for all our sins. Hallelujah!

*"He has made us alive together with Him, having forgiven you all trespasses"* (Colossians 2:13). Jesus forgave all our sins! The word "all" in the above scripture is

the Greek word *"pas,"* meaning "every kind or variety . . . the totality of the persons or things referred to."⁹ It refers to "all, any, every, the whole."¹⁰ So "all" means all. God's forgiveness of our sins covers every sin—past, present, and future! When we received the Lord Jesus as our Savior, we received total and complete forgiveness of all our sins.

*"What shall we say then? Shall we continue in sin that grace may abound? Certainly not! How shall we who died to sin live any longer in it?"* (Romans 6:1-2). This good news is not an excuse to sin but to glorify Jesus for such amazing grace. This good news empowers us to overcome sin. Don't be afraid of God's grace just because someone who is not born again is using it to justify their sinful lifestyle. Remember we don't overcome the devil by trying harder; the Bible says that we overcome him by the blood of the Lamb (Revelation 12:11). *"...And the blood of Jesus Christ His son cleanses us from all sin"* (1 John 1:7).

## Confession Removes Consciousness of Sin

Confessing your sins as a saint has two tremendous benefits: it removes both the guilty consciousness of sin and the dreadful grip that Satan may have over your heart. 1 John 1:9 says, *"If we confess our sins, He is faithful and just to forgive us our sins and to cleanse us from all unrighteousness."*

This does not mean that God will forgive sin only if it has been specifically confessed. So many people live in

⁹ NT: 3956, William Edwy Vine, Vine's Expository Dictionary of Biblical Words. Copyright © 1985, Thomas Nelson Publishers.
¹⁰ NT: 3956, James Strong, Biblesoft's New Exhaustive Strong's Numbers and Concordance with Expanded Greek-Hebrew Dictionary. Copyright © 1994, 2003, 2006 Biblesoft, Inc. and International Bible Translators, Inc.

fear that if they don't confess all their sins before they die, they will not enter into heaven. Confession doesn't give you salvation; Jesus does. Praying a sinner's prayer doesn't save you; Jesus saves you. Salvation comes through a person and His name is Jesus.

When a person repents and believes the Gospel of Jesus Christ, *all* of his sins, past, present and future are immediately forgiven! Christians confess their sins to God to practice humility before Him and to own up to the bad things they have done. Anything you might confess to God does not surprise Him at all because He already knows what you did wrong. It takes a humble person to admit his mistakes! Humility is a vital part that brings restoration to the child of God who has quenched the Holy Spirit.

When we contain sin, it contaminates our soul. Sin neglected makes us infected. Therefore, confessing it removes the consciousness of your sin and failure. God is already aware of what you did wrong, but are you? Are you willing to expose your heart and admit it? When you bring to the light the sin you've been hiding, your conscience gets free again. Confessing your sin is like washing your hands. We all need to do it regularly. Washing your hands is not the same as taking a shower. Sins we pick up on our journey of life are like dirty germs which make us sin. But if we practice regular confession, it will cleanse our soul from those sins.

During the Last Supper before the crucifixion, Jesus washed His disciple's feet, which became such a beautiful picture of our daily cleansing as believers. When Peter objected to his feet being washed, Jesus said to him, *"He who is bathed needs only to wash his feet, but is completely clean; and you are clean, but not all of you"* (John 13:10). "Who is bathed" refers to those who have been saved by trusting in the blood of Jesus which took care of all past, present, and future sin - they have been made completely clean. But, as we walk through life, we pick up so many contaminants in this world and we still need to be washed daily through the washing of God's Word and confessing our wrongdoings. Why? Not so that we can be cleansed again, but, since we are already clean, we need to maintain our daily relationship with Jesus. *"Jesus answered him, 'If I do not wash you, you have no part with Me'"* (John 13:8). Jesus is not just interested in saving us but also in sanctifying us, which takes place through reading and meditating in the Bible and confessing any revealed sin. That's why as believers we have one bath but many washings. It's like this: every day we take one shower, but many times we wash our hands throughout the day.

The Lord uses confession to remove specks of dirt out of the heart just as Jesus removed the dirt off the feet of his followers by washing them with water. When we confess our sin to the Lord, he removes the spiritual blemishes that sin puts on our conscience, our soul.

## Remove the Mask, Remove the Enemy

When Esther entered the banquet hall for the second time, she told the king the truth about her identity and her past. The king who was her husband didn't get angry at her for coming out and revealing the truth about her Jewish ancestry. While sharing her past, she also shared that Haman had plans to exterminate her people, including her. After Esther opened her heart and shared her struggle, the king became furious with her wicked enemy, Haman. Shortly after, that enemy was thrown out of the

banquet hall and hanged on the gallows that he had prepared for Esther's cousin Mordecai.

There is such great power in confessing our sin. When
we remove the mask, God will remove the enemy. When
we become truthful with our struggles, we will experience
freedom. *"You shall know the truth and the truth will set
you free"* (John 8:32). We can only be as free as we are
willing to be truthful. As long as we are hiding, concealing,
blaming, and accusing others, God can't set us free. I am
not saying that God will not love you or accept you, but He
can't help you if you are not going to come clean with what
you are going through.

It's true that God already has forgiven us forever in
Christ. But confessing our sin is essential because it is a
part of the sanctification process which helps us in overcoming our sin. Please, my friend, don't struggle secretly
or suffer silently. Bring that hidden thing out into the
light! I don't mean to post it on Facebook or Instagram or
to message some "man of God" on social media who has
no idea who you are and spill all your beans to him. That's
being weak and timid. Take it to the cross, to Jesus. When
you have sinned, don't hide from God; run to Him.

Follow up your confession to God by going to your
spouse, a trusted mentor, a pastor, or your mom or dad.
Going to someone, when you open yourself up, will cause
your heart to beat faster and your blood to rush. You need
to get real and raw. Then you will see how God will not
only cleanse you but free you from the attraction of that
forbidden fruit. *"Therefore confess your sins to each
other and pray for each other so that you may be healed.
The prayer of a righteous man is powerful and effective"*
(James 5:16). Confessing our sins to others helps us to not
hide them anymore. There is such a relief and cleansing
that takes place when we confess. When we are honest

with our struggles, the pressure to constantly hide or justify ourselves disappears. Being transparent helps us to eliminate our dirty secrets.

Another big reason for confessing our sin is that it breaks the grip of that sin over our lives. Satan is the king of darkness. His works are best done in darkness and sin loses its power in the light. The power of sin is weakened when it's exposed to the light.

Lastly, confession brings healing. As James wrote in chapter 5, we should confess our sins to each other not for forgiveness but for healing. There is emotional healing that is released through confession. Even physical healing can occur because of confessing our sins.

We have to confess our sin to God, to our mentors or accountability partner and to those whom our sin has affected. So, if your sin has affected your spouse, you must ask for forgiveness. Don't wait for them to find out. Just do it out of obedience to the Holy Spirit's conviction.

The mistake that Judas made after committing his gross sin was to confess it to the wrong people. He was the one that Jesus referred to as "not clean" when he washed the disciples' feet. *"For He knew who would betray Him; therefore He said, 'You are not all clean' "* (John 13:11). Judas needed a bath, not just a washing of his feet. He needed conversion, not confession. This is evident because he decided to hang himself for the sin he committed, instead of trusting in the One who was hung for his sin. Every person who doesn't accept Jesus' death on the cross will have to pay for his own sins. Judas didn't need to pay for his sin because his Savoir was already doing that on his behalf. He wanted to return the money he was paid for betraying Jesus. Restitution is good, but if it's not born out of repentance, it doesn't lead to freedom. Although Judas returned the money, he still felt guilty because only

# Fight Back

God gives forgiveness. The Pharisees couldn't give him the gift of forgiveness. In fact, they cared even less about him! No amount of trying to clean up your life will ever bring you peace if you don't get it from Jesus.

If you are not born again, you will be tempted to constantly do good works to outweigh the bad ones. That will never be enough. If good works were enough, then Jesus died in vain. You have fallen short of the glory of God. But God has good news for you. He is offering you the gift of eternal life. You can't earn this gift, you must receive it. To pay for a gift would make that gift void. Accept His gift today. Stop trying; start trusting. Your good works can't erase your bad ones; only Jesus can. In fact, let's pray right now to receive Jesus into your heart. If you believe that He is the Son of God and are ready to repent of your sins and trust in Him, pray along with me out loud,

*"Lord Jesus, I believe that you are the Son of God who came to die on the cross for all my sins. I am a sinner in great need of your mercy and grace. I repent of what I did that offended you and hurt others. Please forgive me for all my wrongdoings. Jesus, come live in me by your Holy Spirit. Give me a new heart and nature. Make me your child today. I receive your gift of a new life right now. Thank you, Jesus. Amen."*

If you prayed that prayer for the first time or are coming back to the Lord, email me so that I may send you some information about developing your new relationship with the Lord. info@vladimirsavchuk.com

Now, if you are born again and have backslidden, or keep on slipping and falling, just trust in God's love for you. The attractions to the world and its sinful fantasies will fade away as you begin to treasure His love for you

# Remove the Mask

more and more. Come back to Jesus! He will cleanse your conscience and restore your soul.

Find someone today to whom you can confess things that have a grip on your soul. I will believe and pray with you for your freedom. What the king did for Esther, Jesus will do for you. Haman will be removed from having access to your palace. While that is great news, removing Haman did not remove the battle.

# Fight Back

## **Thoughts to Share**
*Use #fightbackbook #pastorvlad hashtags.*

Sooner or later what we do in secret will become public.

People get tired of running toward God because it's hard to run with a weight on their back.

Although our spirit is perfect forever, we are continuously being perfected in our soul.

Your sin and failure is not your identity. Jesus is your identity.

If you want to go and sin no more, you must embrace Jesus' gift of "no condemnation."

When we remove the mask, God will remove the enemy.

You are not a son by worth; you're a son by birth.

Chapter 8

# Fight Back

Marizza was raised in a physically, emotionally and verbally abusive home. From the age of 8 until the age of 12, she was molested by a family member. This started a cycle of lustful dreams about being with someone of the same-sex and led her into a path of inner turmoil and confusion. She was greatly distressed and disoriented, not knowing where to go or what to do.

During the next part of her life, Marizza battled with rejection and suicidal thoughts. As time passed things seemed to only get worse as Marizza discovered her father had stage 4 cancer with only a few months to live. Desperate, Marizza sought fulfillment in all the wrong places. The abuse and neglect of all the men in her life distorted her view of how a decent man should be. Abandoning hope in men, Marizza acted on the lustful dreams she had when she was young and entered into her first same-sex relationship. One day she found out that one of her friends committed suicide just before her father passed away. That pushed her to the edge. Losing all direction in life and almost committing suicide, she was eventually admitted into a psych ward.

Even though she was not aware of God's interest in her life, He was always there helping her and giving her hope. Being on a local wrestling team, Marizza met her friend Marylou who later invited her to Hungry Generation Church. Not knowing what she was getting into, Marizza started to attend regularly. She began to notice that the God of the Bible isn't passive and is very much active and alive today. God became very real to her. After she experienced her first deliverance, she started to go through prayer lines multiple times. Step-by-step, during every prayer line she went through, more and more things came off such as the same sex-attraction, suicidal tendencies, shame and past hurts.

Even when she found herself backsliding, the Holy Spirit would always pursue her and call her back to Him. Marizza was like a blind person who could finally see; the veil was lifted. She totally surrendered her life to Jesus and was filled with the Holy Spirit. The Lord became her protector, defender and a father figure she could finally trust and respect.

## The Enemy is Defeated, the Plot is Reversed

*"On that day King Ahasuerus gave Queen Esther the house of Haman, the enemy of the Jews. And Mordecai came before the king, for Esther had told how he was related to her"* (Esther 8:1). The enemy had been defeated and the king gave the house of Haman to Esther. When Jesus died on the cross, He defeated our wicked spiritual enemy for us. *"Having disarmed principalities and powers, He made a public spectacle of them, triumphing over them in it"* (Colossians 2:15).

However, even though Haman had been hanged, his evil plot to destroy all the Jews still remained in effect. *"Now Esther spoke again to the king, fell down at his feet, and implored him with tears to counteract the evil of Haman the Agagite, and the scheme which he had devised against the Jews"* (Esther 8:3). Esther was happy that the enemy was defeated, but now she was pleading with the king to ask him to empower her people to fight back. The king honored her request and letters were sent out giving the Jews a fighting chance.

Now, they were not only celebrating a huge victory over their enemy, but they were authorized to fight from their position of victory against their enemy. *"By these letters the king permitted the Jews who were in every city to gather together and protect their lives—to destroy, kill, and annihilate all the forces of any people or province that would assault them, both little children and women, and to plunder their possessions"* (Esther 8:11). Look at the wording in the letter addressed to the Jewish people. They were permitted to destroy, to kill and to annihilate those who would assault them and to plunder them. I know this is R-rated language and sounds very brutal, but our enemy Satan comes to kill, steal, and destroy, too (John 10:10). Here, Jews were permitted to do to the enemy what the enemy had planned to do to them.

The king not only eliminated the enemy Haman, but he empowered the people to fight the forces still at play even after Haman's demise. The people had an ally in the palace who cheered them on to fight and win. Their enemy was scared because their leader Haman was defeated. The enemy didn't stand a chance if Jews took their proper place. The only way the opposing forces against the Jews would have succeeded was if the Jews had not known of Haman's defeat and had not known that they were authorized to fight back and win. That ignorance would have cost them their victory. The good news which the couriers took to the Jew was that they were empowered. This brought them joy and gladness even before they had to fight. *"The Jews had light and gladness, joy and honor. And in every province and city, wherever the king's command and decree came, the Jews had joy and gladness, a feast and a holiday. Then many of the people of the land became Jews, because fear of the Jews fell upon them"* (Esther 8:16-17).

Satan doesn't want you to know about his defeat and your authority in Christ. He is the king of darkness and darkness is the absence of light. When you live in ignorance, you are easily defeated. It's not because the devil is so powerful, but it's because you are ignorant of how powerful you are in Christ. In this chapter God will use this truth to remove the lies of the enemy concerning you and the devil. I believe that joy, gladness and honor will fill your heart as you learn the truth about how victorious you already are in Christ.

Jesus did more than defeat the enemy. He said, *"I give you the authority to trample on serpents and scorpions, and over all the power of the enemy"* (Luke 10:19). Our enemy has indeed been disarmed and defeated.

## Created for Dominion

We were made in the image of God and created for dominion. *"Then God blessed them, and God said to them, 'Be fruitful and multiply; fill the earth and subdue it; have dominion over the fish of the sea, over the birds of the air, and over every living thing that moves on the earth'"* (Genesis 1:28). God blessed us with the powerful commandment to be fruitful and multiply, to fill the earth and to subdue it. And then there is this part of our spiritual DNA, "have dominion." We were created for dominion, not for deliverance. Because we fail to exercise dominion over the snake, we find ourselves in need of deliverance from the dominion of the enemy. To exercise dominion, we need an enemy. God placed that old serpent under the feet of Adam and Eve. That was a slap in the face of the devil to be put under the authority of human beings who had been existing for only a few days after their creation. Adam and Eve hadn't even been to Heaven. They didn't hear the angels sing. They didn't go to theology school. Dominion over God's enemy who enticed one-third of the angels was given to them. God had so much trust in Adam. God had faith in Eve. We talk about having faith in God, but can I remind you that God had faith in you when He gave you authority and dominion.

Adam and Eve were placed in paradise. This beautiful place also had a snake. Yes, paradise had a parasite. Paradise is not the absence of the enemy, it's having dominion over it. God's view of the good life on earth was not the absence of battle. Blessing is walking in victory and exercising our dominion. Adam's perfect world had a snake in it. And it was still perfect because Adam had dominion. But when Adam disobeyed God, he lost that dominion. Now he came under the dominion of the enemy.

When Jesus, the Son of God, faced the tempter in the wilderness, the devil didn't hide the fact that authority on earth is now his. *"And the devil said to Him, 'All this authority I will give You, and their glory; for this has been delivered to me, and I give it to whomever I wish'"* (Luke 4:5). He declared that all this authority has been delivered to me. Hmmm, I wonder who delivered it to the devil. It wasn't God for sure! *"The heaven, even the heavens, are the Lord's; but the earth He has given to the children of men"* (Psalm 115:16). God gave the earth to His children, the children of men. Of course, God didn't give man ownership over the earth because the earth still belongs to the Lord. *"The earth is the Lord's, and all its fullness, the world and those who dwell therein"* (Psalm 24:1). God was holding the title deed to the earth, but He gave the responsibility and dominion over it to humans. That's why blaming God for what happens on earth is not right.

It's as if your parents give you a car and you wreck it, you can't blame your parents. You might go and ask them for money to fix it, but blaming them after you drove reck-lessly is foolish. Through sin, we give ourselves over to the enemy. We relinquish our dominion and turn ourselves into slaves of sin.

We are either walking in dominion over the devil or living under his dominion of sin. Because we lost our do-minion, we are in need of deliverance. Keep in mind, we were not created for deliverance but for dominion.

Deliverance has become our need because we fail to exercise dominion.

## Dominion is Restored
## Through the Cross

When Jesus delivered us from the grip of the devil, you would think that He wouldn't ever entrust us again with authority since we blew it the first time. You would think that God would *learn* a lesson - don't trust humans with dominion. They don't know what to do with it. Just deliver them and keep them safe until the rapture. Don't trust them to resist deceitful Satan. Don't entrust them to cast out demons. The devil and his demons are cunning and deceitful. If they could manipulate angels into decep-tion, how much more mere humans.

I am going to say it again, God believes in us more than we trust in Him. Because following our deliverance from our past life of sin, Jesus said, *"I saw Satan fall like lightning from heaven. Behold, I give you the authority to trample on serpents and scorpions, and over all the power of the enemy, and nothing shall by any means hurt you"* (Luke 10:18-19). God is immediately trusting us again with authority. His disciples were not mature yet. In fact, they were not baptized in the Holy Spirit yet. Jesus didn't wait for them to finish Bible school before giving them authority. The devil is powerful, but he is not all-powerful! Our enemy has power, but we have authority over all of his power through our Lord Christ Jesus.

*"For if by the one man's offense death reigned through the one, much more those who receive abundance of grace and of the gift of righteousness will reign in life through the One, Jesus Christ"* (Romans 5:17). Satan rules over humanity because of sin, but we can rule over him because of God's gift of righteousness and through the abundance of His grace. Dominion was first given to us at creation, and then Jesus had to restore it on the cross. We are saved by grace through faith, but we are also empowered by grace to reign in life. Many of us appropriate only enough grace to make it to heaven but have not gone for an abundance of grace to reign while here on earth.

Believers today are like the people of Israel who had come out of Egypt but failed to enter the promised land. We have been saved by grace, but now it's time to be empowered by that grace to reign. If you have been delivered from the power of sin, curses and demons, it's time to move on to walk in dominion.

As we see with Esther, the king delivered her life from immediate death and destruction, but she didn't settle for just that. She came requesting authority to have dominion over her enemies and to be able to fight back. The king gave her that permission.

Our king Jesus gives us the gift of righteousness and His sovereign grace to reign in life. Don't settle for just deliverance from sin. Go on to God's original intent for you which is dominion in life. Grace is not given to help us to merely survive, but to thrive.

# Fight Back

## Whatever is Not Removed

You are empowered to resist. Yes, my friend. Whatever God hasn't removed, he has empowered you to overcome. The king removed Haman, but he empowered the Jews to resist the rest of their enemies whom the defeat of Haman did not remove. The ball was now in their court. The choice was theirs. The Jews could have sat around and complained about why the king didn't remove the evil scheme after removing Haman (the edict was irrevocable), or they could take up their place of authority and fight back. And fight back they did!

Maybe in your life, you feel like God has not removed everything you have asked him to remove. Perhaps you are still waiting for God to give you freedom. What if God is waiting for you to start walking in daily victory? What if God has already removed your "Haman," and now He is waiting for you to fight back? What if the reason God is not "delivering" you, even though you escaped from Egypt, is because you are now in the promised land where you are commanded to fight enemies and take their territories?

Jesus said, *"From the days of John the Baptist until now the kingdom of heaven suffers violence and the violent take it by force"* (Matthew 11:12). We are in those days right now, the days of John the Baptist. These are the days when the Lord is building a mighty army of soldiers. Many of us are content to live as babies in spiritual daycare centers. Have you noticed that Jesus said that this mighty army of soldiers will take it by force? They are not waiting for God to give them something first. They have the Holy Spirit who reminds them of what is already theirs in Christ Jesus. Through faith and prayer, they take authority, push back the darkness and advance the kingdom.

# Fight Back

## No Longer a Slave

We used to be slaves to the devil, but after being freed from our spiritual Egypt, we may be tempted to develop a survival mentality. A survival mentality is a victim mindset. We must embrace the calling to be a good soldier of God. *"You, therefore, must endure hardship as a good soldier of Jesus Christ"* (2 Timothy 2:3). Israel couldn't possess the promised land with a victim attitude. In fact, the people who were delivered didn't really understand how God regarded them; they lived like slaves in their minds and died as victims in the wilderness. Of course, they blamed God for their failures. They waited on God to do everything for them. Because they failed to develop into soldiers, they died like slaves even though they were free from Egypt.

In Egypt, they were slaves; in the promised land, they had to be soldiers.

In Egypt, they got deliverance; in the promised land, they had to walk in dominion.

In Egypt, God freed them from Pharoah; in the promised land, God entrusted them with Philistines.

In Egypt, plagues attacked the enemy; in the promised land, they were the plague - their presence brought terror on the nations.

In Egypt, they ran from the enemy; in the promised land, the enemy ran from them.

In Egypt, Moses used the staff; in the promised land, Israel followed the ark.

In Egypt, they asked the Egyptians for things; in the promised land, they simply took them from the Canaanites.

In Egypt, they had bondage; in the promised land, they had battles.

Israel expected God to do in the promised land what He had done in Egypt. But God did not deliver them upon arriving in the promised land. Please hear me; this is important. Instead of moving from deliverance to deliverance, God intends for us to move from deliverance to dominion.

## From Freedom to Fighting

When ten of the spies saw the potential upcoming battles in the promised land, they freaked out. Their view of life after deliverance from Egypt was similar to how some of us view post-deliverance. Now things would be easy and life would be great. Like Israel, they liked the idea of the promised land but hated the fact that giants were dwelling there. Only two of the spies who finally possessed the promised land were Joshua and Caleb. "*But My servant Caleb, because he has a different spirit in him and has followed Me fully, I will bring into the land where he went, and his descendants shall inherit it*" (Numbers 14:24).

Caleb had a different attitude toward battles. He had the spirit of a soldier. He mentally moved from freedom to fighting, from deliverance to dominion. Caleb made up his mind that battles in the promised land were a sign that he was truly free from Egypt. Battles were proof that he was no longer a slave. Israel trusted God for deliverance from Egypt, but now God entrusted Israel with dominion. He gave them enemies to conquer. God has more faith in us than we have in Him. It's a new season. It's time to make the enemy run. It's time not to be afraid of battles. Battles are prerequisites for a breakthrough.

# Fight Back

## From Rod to Ark

Let's look at this transition closely. This shift from deliverance to dominion wasn't easy for the children of Israel because Moses who had brought them deliverance was dead. The manna that had sustained them in the wilderness ceased. Now, they had to rely on the promise, *"As I was with Moses, so I will be with you. I will not leave you nor forsake you"* (Joshua 1:5).

For deliverance, we rely on a "Moses" or a minister, but to exercise our dominion, we have to rely on the Holy Spirit. You can't allow the absence of Moses to shake your faith. The removal of Moses is a sign that God is developing you to become His warrior. In fact, you can't walk in victory if you always rely on your minister or leader who helped you get free.

You are entering a new season in life. You are ready to step into your original calling, dominion, which may not feel good at first. Living by faith is required, not being controlled by feelings. All throughout Israel's deliverance in Egypt, they depended on Moses' rod; then the priests carried God's ark of the covenant on their shoulders through the desert. Deliverance occurred only because someone else carried the anointing. But now you can't walk successfully in dominion through your "promised land" by borrowing from someone else's relationship with God. You have to put that ark of the covenant on your own shoulders. Develop your own times of prayer and fasting. Get into your secret place and discover intimacy with the Holy Spirit.

No one can get into the promised land riding on the anointing of Moses. You can get out of Egypt like that, but living in your own "promised land" or destiny will not happen that way. If relying on men of God enabled you to get out of Egypt, that will not work in the next season of life. A healthy dominion-mentality requires you to rely not on a man but on the Holy Spirit.

When Jesus was on the earth, God's anointing rested on Him. Then He promised that the Holy Spirit would rest upon His Body, the Church, which entered it's promised land when the Holy Spirit descended on all 120 disciples present in the upper room - not just on the apostles or prophets but on every disciple of Jesus. Without a personal relationship with the Holy Spirit, there is no dominion. The Holy Spirit is the ark of the covenant and it's time to carry Him wherever you go. You must realize that the Holy Spirit wants to have a relationship with you, so talk to Him, walk with Him and obey His voice. If life in bondage was the result of being full of demons, then the life of dominion is the result of being filled with the Holy Spirit.

Fighting back is different than receiving freedom. In freedom, someone else helped you to get free, the Moses that God used. But in fighting, you must develop your own personal relationship with the Holy Spirit.

## From Waiting to Working

When Israel was in Egypt, they waited on God for deliverance, but in the promised land, God was waiting for them to take dominion. In Egypt, God did everything for them with minimum participation from them. In the promised land, God did everything with them, expecting maximum participation from them.

After exiting Egypt, they had to wait for the wind to split the Red Sea, but when entering the promised land, God had to wait for them to step into the Jordan River first before He stopped the flow. Part of the promise to Joshua was "*I will give you every place where your foot will tread on*" (Joshua 1:3). I find it interesting that God didn't tell Joshua, "I will give you every place I promised to Abraham, Isaac, and Jacob." Instead, "I will give you every place you yourself tread on." Every place you march over. Every place you crush underfoot. Every place you trample on. That speaks of warfare. That requires dominion.

This may come as a shock, but Israel didn't get what they were promised; they only got what they fought for. Everyone got deliverance from Egypt, but not everyone got dominion in the promised land. Only those who were willing to "tread on", exercise their authority, crush the enemy, wage warfare and fight got something. The same applies to us. "*And from the days of John the Baptist until now the kingdom of heaven suffers violence, and the violent take it by force*" (Matthew 11:12). Paul says to Timothy, "*This charge I commit to you, son Timothy, according to the prophecies previously made concerning you, that by them you may wage the good warfare*" (1 Timothy 1:18). That's why some people don't see prophetic words concerning their destiny come to pass. They assume God will do all the work for them. God gives you prophetic words as a "promised land" to you. Believe it and act. Now it's time to occupy it. A promise from God makes you a potential possessor.

Now it's time to fight from your position of victory to bring it all to reality in the physical realm. Like Israel, we don't fight for victory, but we fight from victory. We fight. In your promised land you don't get what you're promised; you get what you tread on. It's up to you to take possession.

# Fight Back

## From Complaining to Circumcision

After crossing the Jordan River into the promised land, Joshua had all the men of Israel circumcised. That's a painful procedure. Now, compare that with Israel crossing the Red Sea. A few days after that incredible miracle of escaping through the sea, the people who were delivered complained. That was painful for God to hear. The ex-slaves complained, but the soldiers got circumcised.

Complaining brings pain to God; circumcision brings pain to the flesh. God was teaching a new generation that before they can have dominion over their enemy, they must conquer their own flesh by bringing it into subjection. Before we can ever subdue the Canaanites, we must subject our carnal desires to the will of God. That my friend is painful.

*"Thus I fight: not as one who beats the air. But I discipline my body and bring it into subjection, lest, when I have preached to others, I myself should become disqualified"* (1 Corinthians 9.26-27). Paul, who walked consistently in dominion and knew his authority in Jesus, shares his secret routine practice. The discipline of the flesh is required for dominion in the spiritual realm. And he continued, *"...you have taken off your old self with its practices and have put on the new self which is being renewed"* (Colossians 3:9-10).

That's what Joshua commanded his men to do. Before they were about to embark on the battlefield against the enemy, they had to defeat an inner enemy called the flesh. Circumcising of the foreskin removed the *"reproach of Egypt from the camp of Israel"* (Joshua 5:9). Deliverance gets the demons out, but discipline keeps them out. Deliverance is what God does for you; discipline is what God does inside you. Discipline is absolutely essential to walking in dominion. You can't aimlessly watch what you watch, listen to what you listen to, hang out with whom you hang out and still expect to walk in victory. There is a cutting that must take place for those who are called to conquer. Some can't conquer their enemy because their flesh hasn't been cut off. They can't live for the Savior because they are not dead to their "self."

To walk in dominion, we must cut away complaining because complaining is to the devil what worship is to God.

## From Getting to Giving

Another change that must happen in us if we are to fight back victoriously is in the area of giving. Israel serves as a good example for us. What they went through physically, we go through spiritually. Upon leaving Egypt, the people were given valuable gifts, treasures and riches by the Egyptians. That was awesome. But when they entered the promised land, the first thing that God asked His people to do was to give Him the entire city of Jericho and absolutely everything in it. God wanted the first conquest to belong entirely to Him.

The slave mentality is scared of giving; it lives on getting. God wanted to break that poverty way of thinking by teaching His children to exercise the practice of generosity. Poverty runs on fear; provision operates by faith.

It takes faith to give God the entire "city of Jericho." You do the fighting but keep nothing for yourself. Our carnal mind screams, "That's not fair!" Greed in us yells, "It's mine!" Worldliness demands, "I deserve this; I worked so hard for this." A person who is a slave to Mammon (the false god of greed) freaks out at the thought of extravagant generosity. You can't be in dominion if you are a slave to your possessions, wealth, and things. Are you free or are you still a slave?

The primary indication that money owns you is your reluctance to obey God with your money. It's almost like God was trying to break the Israelites away from the slave mentality. He was chipping away at "the victim" thinking. Their mind was being remodeled into thinking like prosperous people. They became generous before they became rich. They were victorious before they won a battle. That's faith.

Shrewd people say, put yourself first; wisdom says, put God first. The world saves first, but the kingdom gives first. In the wilderness, the former slaves used the treasures they brought from Egypt to build a golden calf to worship, but in the promised land, they gave an entire city in worship to the Creator. It's not about money; it's all about your mindset. Greed is the slave of fear; generosity is the distinguishing mark of spiritual soldiers. One of the ways dominion works is demonstrated in the way we handle finances. We can't walk in dominion if we are slaves to the greedy spirit Mammon. Period.

Walking in dominion is more than rebuking the devil. It's giving your income to the Lord as a way to honor Him. When you give Him your income, you're giving Him of yourself who earned that income.

## From Monuments to Memorials

When the children of Israel entered the Promised Land, God commanded them to take twelve stones from the river Jordan and build a memorial on the river bank. *"Then you shall answer them that the waters of the Jordan were cut off before the ark of the covenant of the*

# Fight Back

*Lord; when it crossed over the Jordan, the waters of the Jordan were cut off. And these stones shall be for a memorial to the children of Israel forever"* (Joshua 4:7).

Those who fight and walk in dominion must learn to build memorials to God's many miracles in their life, not monuments to unanswered questions. Every time God does something spectacular in your life, you must take "a stone" from that situation and build a memorial in your mind. That memory becomes a point of reference for your faith when things get hard. We all go through our "Jordan Rivers" in life. Sometimes we go through very low points in our journey of faith, but God never leaves us there in despair. He gets us through. So, take stones from those points of life as a reminder of God's faithfulness to you.

When the Jews left Egypt and wandered in the wilderness, they kept remembering the fish they ate freely in Egypt, the cucumbers, the melons, the leeks, the onions and the garlic (Numbers 11:5). They remembered only the good things they had enjoyed in the land of Egypt. They kept wanting to return because they had monuments or memories in their mind about the land of Egypt. They seemed to forget about all the decades of suffering they had experienced there. They totally forgot about the signs and wonders that God had performed to get them out. All they could remember were onions, cucumbers, garlic and melons. They had a severe case of amnesia to the miracles that God did and to the way He delivered them out of the hellish life in slavery. Instead, they remembered the wrong stuff.

They had just crossed the Jordan River and were about to take possession of the promised land by fighting instead of just waiting. God gave them a little homework to do first. He ordered them to build a memorial to the incredible miracle they had witnessed at the river Jordan.

# Fight Back

God wanted their mindset to be built on His marvelous works. When they faced the walls of Jericho and when the manna stopped, we don't see the Israelites reminiscing about the good old days in the wilderness of Egypt. They were strong in the faith because they now were focused on the extraordinary works that God had done for them in the past.

Fighting comes from faith. Faith comes from remembering God's faithfulness. Yes, faith comes from the hearing of God's Word (Romans 10:17), but it also comes from remembering God's works (Joshua 4:6-7). One of the reasons people go from deliverance to deliverance instead of deliverance to dominion is they don't have faith. They live by their feelings. They are controlled by symptoms. They bring God down to the level of their moods. God's Word is no more important to them than their feelings about what they see happening in their lives. A person who wants to walk in dominion must live by faith, not by sight. A life of faith is not that hard. It's based on feeding yourself with God's Word and remembering God's works.

If we don't build a memorial to what God did, the devil will hijack our mind by filling it with what God did not do. Instead of building memorials to miracles, we build monuments to unexplained doubts and questions. Why didn't God prevent this accident from happening to me? Why didn't God heal my friend or loved one? Why, oh God, did someone commit suicide after we prayed for him? Why wasn't this or that prayer answered? Why was I born this way? These are mysteries that plague our minds. For some of those questions, we will never get answers on this side of eternity. Questions are normal, but building monuments to things that God has not done or was expected to do will weaken our faith. Once our faith is crippled, it's hard to be victors. We fall into self-pity and live like a victim.

In this broken world, if you want to walk in dominion, you must intentionally remember what God has done in your life. Remember His miracles, all the answered prayers, all the fulfilled dreams, all the things He delivered you from. Put into your memory bank all the gifts that He graciously gives you each day, which usually you take for granted. And don't forget what He did on the cross for your eternal salvation and on the day of Pentecost when He sent his Spirit to dwell in you. You have to build into your soul an archive of God's faithfulness. Design your memorial in your mind and heart; otherwise, your mind will gravitate naturally by default to all the things that God did not do.

Some of us live in a constant state of recalling what God has not done. Others live remembering what they haven't done yet or what they did do that was wrong. For example, when Jesus taught His disciples to stay away from the leaven of religious leaders, he was referring to the teachings of religious people. *"Then Jesus said to them, 'Take heed and beware of the leaven of the Pharisees and the Sadducees'. And they reasoned among themselves, saying, 'It is because we have taken no bread.' "* (Matthew 16:6-7). To the disciples, the word leaven made them think of what they didn't do. They forgot to take bread with them for their journey. Then Jesus kindly rebukes them for their little faith. I find it interesting that Jesus then goes on to remind them of the fantastic miracle of multiplying loaves of bread and fish. In fact, He reminded them of both times that miracle took place in order to help them to better understand. Even if they did forget the loaves, the Miracle Maker was with them in their boat. Why didn't they remember that He is able to do it again and again? I am like those disciples. When something goes bad, I find myself thinking about what I did wrong instead of what Jesus did right. It's easy to let our mind go wild in the direction of our past mistakes. But as Jesus' disciples, we must look back into our past to see what Jesus did right, not focus on what we failed to do. Otherwise, we will operate on "little faith."

On your most difficult days, remember what God has already done, how He saved you and has healed you. Whenever things get hard for me, what keeps me from falling into fear is that I remember the many milestones in my life. I remember immigrating to the United States. I remember how I didn't enjoy my teenage years because I was bound by porn and insecurity. I remember how anxious I was around people. I remember how we obtained a building for our church without money and documents. That was supernatural. I remember how when I was a youth pastor, I struggled for ten years with a youth group that didn't grow. I remember how I had difficulties in the first few years of my marriage. However, when I remember all that God did in spite of my problems, my faith rises up and I refresh in my mind all the prophetic words that God has given me. Then my faith is strengthened; I feel like a spiritual giant. I can take on anything that comes my way. Learn to build memorials out of memories in your mind. Don't let your mind gravitate to what is wrong with you, how your life sucks, and God didn't do this and didn't do that. If you let your mind go there, you will live as a slave to your circumstances instead of your calling to be a victorious soldier.

If you can't think of any great things in your past that God has done, remember the cross and Pentecost. Remember other people's testimonies that you have heard. In the back of my mind, I have a list of testimonies from our church that I recall when things get hard in my ministry and everyday life. For example, there was a guy who overdosed four times and was declared dead, but today he is the head usher in our church. Praise God! Or, there was a young girl who was totally paralyzed from the neck down due to an accident, but now she is free and totally healed. And the list goes on and on. I am the one who chooses what my mind dwells on. I don't allow the enemy to use my feelings, mood, or situations to build a monument to fear, unbelief and depression. Let's build memorials, not monuments.

## No More Manna

When you walk in dominion and victory, God stops the manna. Oh, this is scary for the people who have a slave mentality. Manna was God's provision in the desert; it was just enough to make it through. It was God's blessing for that season in the wilderness, but it was not His ultimate promise. God promised His people milk and honey. Manna was only a temporary provision; milk and honey were God's ultimate promise. It's possible to get so accustomed to the plain, ordinary manna in life that we forget what God has really promised us. When the manna is taken away, we tend to panic, get scared, look for what we did wrong and complain to God as to why He took away something that He gave us in the first place.

I don't see the children of Israel doing that in the promised land. They kept their eyes on the promise of God when the temporary blessings (which had lasted for forty years) ceased. They knew God wouldn't take away the manna without bringing something better into their lives. God doesn't remove something good if he doesn't plan to bless you with something better. That knowledge came from the promise that God made to their forefathers Abraham, Isaac, and Jacob.

We have to train our spirit to remember God's promises and prophetic words when good things stop. It's like when God led Elijah to a brook that provided water for him during a drought, but then the brook dried up. But Elijah didn't despair. He listened to the Holy Spirit direct him to a widow's house. When your brook dries up, God's river is always full of water. When your manna stops, God is setting you up to enjoy the milk and honey of the promised land. When someone leaves your circle of friends, God is getting ready to bring in somebody better. Maybe you lost a job or business even though you're walking in victory; that means God is preparing you for His milk and honey.

Jesus told us in John 15 that pruning happens to the branch that is bearing fruit. Pruning is intended for producing more fruit. But when you are being pruned, it doesn't feel like God is preparing you for more fruit. Pruning feels like punishment. During pruning, all the sucker branches are removed. The branch may look naked and small, but the master knows what he is doing. He is not punishing the branch, but he is preparing it for a greater harvest. That's how you have to view your trials when you go through the loss of manna, when your brook dries up, or when you get pruned. A greater harvest is coming. Something better is on its way. Take courage. Don't quit or fall back into self-pity. Instead, fight back and be powerful. My brother has a bow because he loves to go shooting arrows. I have learned from him that when an archer pulls the arrow back in the bow-string, it's only to release it forward with potential force and power. When things get hard, remind yourself that you are the arrow and your

# Fight Back

God is the archer; your setback is just a set up for a come-back.

## Advance Not Retreat

No more manna doesn't mean that God has left you; it means that God is preparing you for what He has promised. It's part of the process of walking in dominion, learning to see negative things through the eyes of faith. God was building a man of valor out of Gideon and when his army shrank, God told him to advance, not retreat. For an ordinary person that would be a sign to go back home, not move forward. But Gideon was a fighter; he went forward, not backward. Gideon was a man of faith, not a person of fear.

I remember when things were really difficult in our ministry, morale was down. We couldn't get anyone to do anything voluntarily. People weren't getting saved and we didn't see water baptisms for a long time. There was no momentum, revival, or life in the ministry. I was in my early twenties, and I was afraid that my ministry which had hardly begun was already over. People were leaving our church like crazy. The church was shrinking. I felt like my future was shrinking as well. But the Lord spoke to me, and I remember it as clear as day. While I was driving from Pasco to Richland, He said, "Advance. Don't Retreat." I wondered, how can I go forward if my army is shrinking? I don't have the right strategy. I don't have the proper tools. But God's answer was, "Things I promised you when you had nothing will happen not by your might or power, but by My Spirit. Therefore, move forward." I remembered God's faithfulness to me and His promises, and one day at a time I moved forward. Whenever I look back at those days, I am so glad that I didn't fall back, but I fought back.

# Fight Back

## Planted, Not Buried

When thinking about how Jesus was going through an extremely agonizing time on the cross, I love His perspective on His suffering. "*Most assuredly, I say to you, unless a grain of wheat falls into the ground and dies, it remains alone; but if it dies, it produces much grain*" (John 12.24). Jesus' death looked like a burial but He said it was a planting. Jesus was the seed that was thrown into the ground. His friend betrayed Him. His disciples forsook Him. Religious leaders gossiped about Him. Romans soldiers nailed Him to the cross. He died and some friends buried Him. But God planted Him and He rose from the dead. Now over the last twenty centuries, He produced an incredible harvest of saved people.

What applies to Jesus also applies to you and me since we imitate Him. Jesus is not only our Master but also our model. As the Master, Christ suffered for my sin, but as my model, he showed me how to suffer.

Grain seed is extremely small in size. Everything great in life starts with a small seed. Even human life starts with a seed. Don't underestimate small things. Don't regard yourself as worthless just because you are small. The size of the small seed does not dismay the farmer; he doesn't view the seed as invaluable or insignificant. The harvest is hidden in the seed. The forest is in the seed. There is greatness in small things.

How can a small seed be made into a great harvest? The seed must be thrown into the dirt. The seed must be covered by dirt. The seed will be in darkness for a while. The seed will be trampled under the foot of man. The seed must die. That is the process through which the seed must go to become a great harvest. There are no shortcuts. We want the end result without the process. You can't have the crown without the cross. You can't have roses without thorns and resurrection without death. It's not possible.

For you to go from being a small seed to a great harvest, the same thing that happened to the seed has to happen to you. You will be thrown down. You will be surrounded by dirt, unpleasant circumstances. You will be for a moment surrounded by darkness, feeling like God doesn't care and has forsaken you. You will be walked on by people who say things about you, gossiping, backstabbing and doing things that hurt. It will look like you're dying and seem like you're getting buried. But rejoice, because you're only getting planted.

When you feel like you're being buried, remember you're being planted.

Keep a prophetic perspective on your current situation.

Trust in God's plan when it feels like it's a part of the devil's plot.

Rely on the farmer - your heavenly Father - not on your feelings.

A seed is not like a corpse; it has life. You have the life of Jesus living inside of you. No matter what dirt, darkness, or rejection by people surrounds you right now and if it feels like you're being buried, remember you're only being planted. God did not forsake you; He planted you. You will become a forest. You will win. You will possess your possession.

*"He shall be like a tree planted by the rivers of water that bring forth its fruit in its season whose leaf also shall not wither and whatever he does shall prosper"* (Psalm 1:3).

# Fight Back

## **Thoughts to Share**
*Use #fightbackbook #pastorvlad hashtags.*

Jesus' death on the cross defeated and disarmed the devil.

God's goal for humanity was dominion, not deliverance.

God has more faith in you than you will ever have in Him.

Whatever is not removed, you are empowered to overcome.

God wants you to move

- from freedom to fighting,

- from deliverance to dominion,

- from bondage to battle,

- from being a slave to being a soldier.

We are either walking in dominion over the devil or living under his dominion of sin.

Instead of moving from deliverance to deliverance, God intends for us to move from deliverance to dominion.

Battles are proof that we are no longer slaves.

A life in bondage is the result of being full of demons; a life of dominion is the result of being filled with the Holy Spirit.

Israel didn't get what they were promised; they got only what they fought for.

# Fight Back

To walk in dominion we must:

- rely more on God than on man

- work with God instead of waiting on God

- replace whining with worship

- break poverty thinking by being generous

- remember what God has done, not what He hasn't

Don't settle for manna when God has promised milk and honey.

God doesn't remove something good if he doesn't plan to bless you with something better.

Pruning is not punishment; it's a preparation for a greater harvest.

My setback is a set up for a comeback.

If it feels like you're being buried, remember you're only being planted.

Appendix 1

# How to Get Saved

*"Believe on the Lord Jesus Christ, and you will be saved,"* (Acts 16:31).

Before you can believe in Jesus as your Savior, you need to know what you need to be saved from. An umbrella saves you from getting wet. A helmet saves you from getting hurt. Jesus can save you from the punishment and the power of your sin.

Each one of us has sinned against God (Romans 3:23). Even if we try to be really good, we still fall short of God's perfect standard. We sin against God every day by not obeying His commands in the Bible, such as loving Him, honoring our parents and telling the truth.

God is holy (perfect and separate from sin), and He will punish unbelieving sinners by separating them to a place of eternal death and torment called hell. *"For the wages of sin is death, but the gift of God is eternal life in Jesus Christ our Lord"* (Romans 6:23). Due to God's great love, He sent His own Son Jesus to save believers from this punishment by dying on the cross in their place. Then Jesus rose from the dead, proving His victory over sin and death.

*"If you confess with your mouth the Lord Jesus and believe in your heart that God has raised Him from the dead, you will be saved. For with the heart one believes unto righteousness, and with the mouth, confession is made unto salvation" (Romans 10:9-10).*

170

# How to Get Saved

If you would like to receive Jesus Christ and His salvation, please pray this prayer:

*"I come to You, Jesus, to give You my heart and my life. I confess You as the Lord of my life, instead of myself. I ask You to forgive me of my sins and make me clean. I ask this because I believe You paid the price for every wrongdoing and sin I've ever committed. I now receive into my heart Your righteousness and declare that I am saved, and Your child!"*

Welcome to the family of God and your new life in Christ! Please let me know if you have given your life to Jesus by emailing me at info@vladimirsavchuk.com.

*Appendix 2*

# Study Guide

## Introduction
## Deliverance is not the Goal

**Engage:** What is your biggest fear?

## Discussion Questions:

1. Read Psalm 149:6-9; what do these verses mean to you?
2. According to Psalm 149:6-9, what is the honor that believers have? To whom does this honor belong?
3. If God doesn't remove something you are fighting with after you asked him to, what should you do?

## Application:
Take a stand against every unnatural fear and night terror in your life and command it to go in Jesus' name.

# Study Guide

## Chapter 1
## Battles That Didn't Start with You

**Engage:** What character and physical traits got passed down to you from your parents?

## Discussion Questions:

1. What lesson did you learn from Iveta in the incident with her dead grandmother?
2. Read Deuteronomy 28:1-14. (Each member read a few verses.)
   What are the causes for the blessing of God?
   What are the signs of those blessings?
3. Read Deuteronomy 28:15-68. (Each member read a few verses.)
   What are the causes for curses?
   What are the signs of curses?
4. Read Galatians 3:13. Why did Jesus die on the cross? What is promised to Christians today instead of curses?

## Application:
If you notice things like chronic sickness, fears, divorce, poverty, addictions, premature death, or accident tendencies going on in your family, take time this week to pray against it and proclaim the opposite.

## Chapter 2
## Authority Trumps Access

**Engage:** Have you ever had a roommate or rented a room from someone who owned the house?

## Discussion Questions:

1. Read Ephesians 4:27-30. Based on these verses and your experience, what are some of the ways that we can give access to the enemy?
2. Can a Christian be demon-possessed? What is the difference between possessed and oppressed?
3. What are some of the traditional teachings you have heard that caused you to not walk in authority?
4. Read this verse, Luke 10:18. What does this say about our authority?
5. What lesson did you learn from the story of the demon-possessed man and about how much power we have over the enemy?
6. From the story of Lazarus, how important is it to walk even while we are bound?

## Application:
Every morning this week apply the armor of God in prayer before you start your day.

## Chapter 3
## Spiritual Weapons

**Engage:** What was your class graduation-song?

## Discussion Questions:

1.  What lesson did you learn from Paulius' testimony?
2.  What are the four weapons mentioned in chapter three?
3.  Share how prayer and fasting have helped you to gain victory.
4.  Read together Revelation 12:11. What are three ways we can gain access over the enemy?
5.  How can we practically apply the blood of Jesus over our life?
6.  How can fight intrusive thoughts from the devil?

## Application:
Take one day this week to fast and focus on your prayer time. During the time that you would be having a meal, take that time to go into the Word and pray.

## Chapter 4
## Royalty in Rags

**Engage:** Do you like shopping? What's your favorite store to shop at?

## Discussion Questions:

1. What lesson did the story of Hiroo Onoda teach us?
2. Read Romans 12:2. What comes before the transformation of life? What comes before renewing your mind?
3. What are the two keys to renewing our minds?
4. What happens when we have the armor, but we don't wear it?
5. How can one put on the armor of God?
6. Why is it important to come to God's presence "dressed up"?

## Application:

Find three scriptures that would apply to an area in your life where you feel you need the most help. Read the scripture, write the scripture, and speak the scripture over yourself/life. Do this once daily, every day this week.

# Study Guide

## Chapter 5
## Warfare in the Wilderness

**Engage:** What was your favorite topic in school?

## Discussion Questions:

1. What was the difference between Queen Vashti and Queen Esther?
2. Why is a ministry to the Lord so important?
3. How can we get our first love back?
4. What should we do if we don't feel hunger for God?
5. What promise do we have for those who pursue God even if they don't feel like it?
6. How did Jesus respond in the wilderness differently from the nation of Israel?
7. When the teacher is silent, what are we to do?

## Application:
Ask yourself, am I hungry for God? Assess yourself and be honest: if the answer is no, know that simply wanting to be hungry for God is a step in the right direction! Take some time to pray for one another. Ask God to stir up a hunger for the Lord that you cannot ignore.

## Chapter 6
## Seek His Face More Than Freedom

**Engage:** What did you want to be when you grew up?

## Discussion Questions:

1. Why do we sometimes become complacent after receiving freedom from bondage?
2. Read Psalm 149:4. What are some ways we can allow God to enjoy our presence?
3. Read Psalm 100:4. How can we prepare a banquet for the king? Why should we not go looking all the time for "open doors" in our past?
4. Why can't we allow enemies at our table to keep us from eating in the presence of the King?

## Application:
Take time to repent and ask the Holy Spirit to adjust your motives and heart's desire toward Him.

# Study Guide

## Chapter 7
## Removing the Mask

**Engage:** What was your favorite hiding place when you were a kid?

## Discussion Questions:

1. What are some steps we can take to walk in freedom and discernment?
2. Why do you think so many people are hesitant to confess sin?
3. Read 1 John 1:9 and James 5:16. Based on these two verses why should we confess our sins?
4. Was there a time you confessed a sin to God or a leader? If so, how did you feel afterward?
5. What are some habits we can develop to grow spiritually?

## Application:
Set aside a date and time this week to be one-on-one with God.
Acknowledge your sin to Him.
Write a letter to God about your day.

## Chapter 8
## Fight Back

**Engage:** What is your go-to snack?

## Discussion Questions:

1. Why do we need deliverance to exercise dominion?
2. Read Numbers 14:24. What are some battles in your life you feel God is asking you to fight and overcome?
3. Why is it important to develop your relationship with the Holy Spirit in order to exercise dominion?
4. Why is discipline so essential to walking in dominion?

## Application:
Ask the Holy Spirit to reveal the areas in your life that you need to take dominion over.

*Appendix 3*

# About the Author

Vladimir Savchuk is a rising spiritual voice that God is using to profoundly impact this generation. Leveraging modern media technology to propagate the timeless truth of the faith, Pastor Vlad has written books, hosted conferences and created content platforms that are touching hundreds and thousands of people all around the world.

Pastor Vlad's creative approach in leading Hungry Generation church has been used by the Holy Spirit to cultivate an anointed internship program and a worship culture with worldwide reach. He is a gifted speaker with an emphasis on rarely-addressed spiritual topics such as spiritual warfare, deliverance and the Holy Spirit. Pastor Vlad is declaring ancient truths in a modern way.

He is married to his beautiful wife, Lana, with whom he enjoys spending time and doing ministry together.

*Appendix 4*

# Online School

*Then He said to His disciples, "The harvest truly is plen-*
*tiful, but the laborers are few. Therefore pray the Lord*
*of the harvest to send out laborers into His harvest."*
Matthew 9:37-38

In 2020, we launched an online school to impact the world by training up the laborers for God's harvest field. Many believers around the world don't have the time to go to Bible school or can't afford Bible training. Therefore, we make our online school totally free.

Vlad's school consists of courses that are Spirit-filled, practical and scriptural. Powerful topics such as Deliverance, Holy Spirit, Prayer, Ministry, Identity in Christ, etc. All of our classes are offered for free thanks to the generous support of our partners.

Enroll today (www.vladschool.com) to grow in the Lord and to be trained in ministry.

# Stay Connected

Facebook.com/vladhungrygen

Twitter.com/vladhungrygen

Instagram.com/vladhungrygen

YouTube.com/vladimirsavchuk

www.vladimirsavchuk.com

www.vladschool.com

If you have a testimony from reading this e-book, please email info@vladimirsavchuk.com

If you wish to post about this book on your social media, please use tag @vladhungrygen and use #pastorvlad #fightbackbook hashtag.

If you are looking for other books, audio sermons, study guide for small groups, you can find it at www.vladimirsavchuk.com

CPSIA information can be obtained
at www.ICGtesting.com
Printed in the USA
LVHW081526210323
742157LV00004B/422

9 781087 913414